Here's the oak. As a boy
I hid there, held its limbs
and loved its wood.

I once climbed in clouds
up to that bough and learned
intimacy with rain.

Fred (Oak) Offutt
1941–1977

For My Sisters and Brothers

RUNE MAGIC

RUNE MAGIC

The Celtic Runes
as a Tool for Personal
Transformation

DEON DOLPHIN

NEWCASTLE PUBLISHING CO., INC.
North Hollywood, California
1987

CONTENTS

ACKNOWLEDGMENTS

This is the second edition of *Rune Magic*. The first was a small paperback book of forty pages, self-published in 1982. It was beautifully designed and executed by Jane Dill. Only 1,000 copies were printed and the book sold out early in 1985. Rune Magic seems to have been channeled through me by the ancient Goddesses and Druid Masters. Both the book and system of divination were developed through a combination of runic exploration and intuitive speculation.

My deepest thanks to Al Saunders of Newcastle Publishing for giving me the opportunity to write this second edition. A very special thanks to Hank Stine, my editor, for believing in this book and for his patience; and to Riley K. Smith for his beautiful and tasteful artistic presentation of this book. Another special thanks to Danaan Parry, whose words of wisdom helped to set the tone for *Rune Magic*.

Special thanks to Michael and Kirby Odawa for their editorial assistance and for helping me to stay focused; to Marianne Haissman, for her special knowledge of the fields of Jungian and Transpersonal Psychology, and to Jeff and Jai for their loving input. Special thanks also to Philip Wayne for his timely consultations, his songs and for his programming assistance for an upcoming *Rune Magic* software package. Many thanks to Lori Laube for her excellent word processing, and to Rose Farrington for her loving sense of humor and her never-failing belief in this book. Thanks also to Avon Mattison for her clarity, her insights and for helping me find the peace within myself; to Dr. John Perry for his encouragement and wisdom; to John Paul Carobus for his belief that a few stones can share wisdom; to Jeanine Kagan for all her loving support; and to Michel Henry for her encouragement and faith in me.

Thanks to Susie Bonnell and Lynne White for giving me the space to write, and a special thanks to Anthony, Steve and Michael of Publishing on Demand, Inc., without whose support I could not have finished this work on time.

I especially wish to thank Peter Caddy and all the people who have so willingly allowed me to use their rune readings in this book, along with all those who have come to me over the years at the Renaissance Faires. Thanks also to Phyllis Patterson and the staff at the Living History Center for allowing me to participate as "Dame Deone" in the Faire.

I also wish to thank Frank Evans, Carol Gallacci, Joseph and Nathan of CCC in Tiburon, California for their constant wisdom and inspiration. I also thank the good people at the San Francisco Jungian Library for their assistance in this project.

My very special thanks to Donald Fenn for all his love and belief in me. And a most special thanks to my wonderful daughter, Amara Felice, for growing into the beautiful goddess I always knew she was.

Without the support of all of the above, as well as many friends I did not have space to mention by name, this book would not be in your hands.

INTRODUCTION

There is a hill called Newgrange that overlooks the Boyne Valley in Ireland. This hill was created by the predecessors of the Celts 3,000 years ago. They made it into a perfect hyperbola, carrying chunks of quartz crystal from the Wicklow Mountains, a hundred miles away. A slim passageway leads down into this megalithic temple and ends at a threefold chamber where a triple-spiral is carved into the rock. Other rocks are embellished with runes and chevrons. At midwinter solstice, and only then, a shaft of light enters the passageway, and for seventeen minutes each year the chamber is illuminated with glowing light.

A few years ago, at the culmination of an initiation, I sat in that chamber at midwinter solstice. As the light cut through the year-long darkness, it bounced off the triple-spiral, bathed my body and illumined the Celtic rune designs so that they burned into my collective memory. It was a moment in which I knew that the past is not simply a collection of historic facts, a musty list of how-not-to-do-it-again. The past holds wisdom. It is an incredible well of collective knowing that, at certain times in our unfolding, comes to the surface; a primordial wisdom stored within the subconscious mind of every human being on this planet.

The keys to bringing this universal, timeless wisdom up to the level of our conscious awareness are the symbols and rituals that have endured the coming and going of cultures.

When I choose to cast the runestones, it is as if I am knocking on some ancient door. And it is very important for me to remember that the door is inside myself, not separate from me. Somehow the act itself evokes internal wisdom.

Of course, it is possible to go through the motions of casting runes, mindlessly peruse the connected reading and totally waste time. But to set the stage, within and without, to prepare my subconscious to tap into universal wisdom, to quiet my mind and open my heart to my own ability to know-more-than-I-understand, this then creates the wisdom of possibility that transforms a simplistic act into a sacred ritual. Without ever referring to a book, without switching my consciousness from knowing to understanding, from feeling to thinking, I experience my connection with something very old in me, very powerful, very solid. I have knocked on that ancient door, and what shows itself on the other side of the doorway will, I know, be exactly what I need to hear to facilitate the next step in my journey in consciousness.

I thank you, Deon, for molding this ancient "door-knocker" into such a usable tool for our lives today.

Danaan Parry, Director
Holyearth Foundation and
the Earthstewards Network

PREFACE

At a garage sale seven years ago, a small pouch of "Druid Rune Stones" caught my eye and I bought them without really knowing what they were. The pouch contained eleven tiny stones marked with symbols and a card with short runic definitions. At home I found a special handkerchief which I used as a casting cloth. I began doing short readings for myself and my friends and discovered how well the stones worked as a tool of divination.

Six months later a friend suggested that I audition for the local Renaissance Faire. I was offered a booth with the promise that I research the real Viking runes, as the ones I had were not authentic. Odin, the Norse god of the runes, hung for nine nights and days on the Yggdrasil (the Tree of Life) to learn the meaning of the runes, and I feared I would have to do the same.

Marcia Gilfillin, who had studied the runes in the Linguistics Department at the University of Copenhagen, came to my rescue. She brought me a book, *English Runes*, in which I found all the original Anglo-Saxon runic verses. Since that time, I have let the runes guide me. Of course, I never dreamed where these original eleven stones would lead. It has been an exciting and fascinating journey so far and it has only just begun.

My task became to research the runes to discover their ancient origins and to help revive an ancient system of self-communication that had been buried under the debris of the Dark and Middle Ages. In the process, I have been blessed with the opportunity to look far back into history and mythology and to reach deeply within myself. By rekindling the spark of the ancient runes with the dawning light of the Aquarian Age, I have developed a contemporary system for using the runes which I call Rune Magic.

Rune Magic has been my constant teacher. It has taught me the many lessons of the individual runes, each one both a meditation in its own right and a lesson to be put into practice in daily life. This was true both in the development of the original system and in the writing of this book. It has also taught me patience, discipline and self-understanding.

In this book I tell you all the practical ways of using the runes to help improve the quality of your own life, and even how to order a set if you wish. But my hope is that you will be inspired to find and make your own runestones. Bless them, hold them, feel them and look at them; let them speak to you. Discover that within yourself which can allow you to hear and know the runes.

Deon Dolphin
April 1987

CHAPTER I

THE RUNES: AN ANCIENT ORACLE OF SELF-KNOWLEDGE

We merely dream, we only rise from
a dream; it is all as a dream . . .
—W. B. Yeats

THE RUNES AND DIVINATION

The *I-Ching*, the Tarot and the runes are all forms of ancient oracles—devices used as mirrors to catch glimpses of the interactions between our deepest selves and the events of daily life. The *I-Ching* arose out of the wisdom of the ancient Chinese philosophers, the Tarot from a combination of the teachings of the Kabbalah and Egyptian mysticism. The runes are the only oracle of distinctively Western origin. Although each system is used quite differently, they all originate from one common source: the Divine Wisdom, or Logos, in the form of Thoth, Hermes and Odin.

Although the runes have primarily been thought of in popular fancy as nothing more than mysterious symbols, an ancient alphabet carved into large stones, they have been also used in divination. This aspect of the runes was kept secret throughout most of what we know of their history. Rune casters, or *Vitkas*, passed down their knowledge orally, and it was believed that if someone talked or wrote publicly about the runes they would die.

What makes the runes different from any other modern mind game is that they are deeply rooted in the earth's history. Like other oracles, when the runes were used correctly, as a form of blessing and divination, they remained available. When they were misused, they went underground. That they may have roots in our most ancient civilizations suggests the potential depth of their wisdom.

Like seeds planted deep in the earth during the Middle Ages and left dormant over the centuries, the runes are once again sprouting. Just within the past decade, and especially within the past five years, the runes have been flowering independently in many parts of the Western world. Because of the availability of knowledge and speed of communication, each piece of runic information builds upon the other. For the first time in history, the runes are being written about safely and offered to the public as a positive system of divination.

The word "rune" means "mysterium" or "secrets" and refers to glyphic symbols which are said to have originated with the ancient Scandinavian and North Germanic cultures, but which may be of even older origin. The runic alphabet is called the "Futhorc" (pronounced *Foo-thork*), an acronym of the first six runic characters. The word "rune" also refers to sets of verses written about each rune which illuminate its meaning.

At the very least, the runic symbols each represent a concept useful to life. The meanings assigned to the individual runes, as with all early languages and petroglyphs, were derived from a combination of familiar symbols drawn from nature, legend and daily living. The earliest runes were based on the Norse legends of the gods Odin, Tyr and Ing, and the tree spirits, Birch or Poplar (*beorc*) (ᛒ), Yew (*eoh*) (ᛇ), Oak (*ac*) (ᚫ) and Ash (*aesc*) (ᚨ). Other runes represent spiritual states and emotional attitudes.

Runes were first carved into rocks, metal, bone and wood, and later into belt buckles, rings, bracelets, amulets, caskets and on Viking ships in elaborate decorative designs. Throughout Scandinavian countries, and all the countries in which the Vikings traveled, stood large monoliths inscribed with runic epitaphs and messages. Many of these stones were destroyed during the Crusades and the Christianization of Europe. However, some still exist and have been grist for runic scholars since the Eighteenth century. The runes seem to have been spread from the Scandinavian countries into Germany by the Vikings. The Vikings also brought the runes to Iceland, where the Norse Sagas were written down in runic form.

We don't know all the ways in which the runes have been used, but we do know that they were often cast as an oracle. One method for doing so (according to the Roman historian Tacitus, writing in 98 A.D.) was to break a branch from a fruit tree or oak tree, and cut it into sections. Then the runes were marked on these pieces and cast onto a cloth. After a prayer to the gods, the *Vitka*, or rune-caster, would draw a sacred circle on the ground, cast the runes into the circle and interpret their meaning.

The runes, as used in *Rune Magic*, are not a fortune-telling device, but rather a method of reading the present-time patterns in a person's life, although both past and future may be seen in the context of readings. This makes the runes an ideal tool for communicating with the inner self. Through casting and interpreting the runes, we discover new ways of viewing the forces within ourselves and new ways of using these energies to resolve the problems in our lives. For just as Odin attained enlightenment while seeking the secret of the runes, so we can attain enlightenment, using the wisdom of the runes as a guide.

By showing the differences in our individual natures without passing judgment, the runes can help us learn to know ourselves and one another more clearly and fully. The runes are a good way of straightening out relationships between lovers, and even of resolving lovers' quarrels. The runes, as a tool of communication, offer a means for family members to begin to better understand one another. They work wonderfully with teenagers, especially those who have played the game, "Dungeons and Dragons." They are also an effective and delightful means for therapist and client to get to know each other.

The runes can also be an excellent vehicle for learning to balance opposites. Some of the runic symbols represent the polarities and dualities in life which we must balance in order to experience peace and harmony. These include: male/female, hero/fool, conflict/clarity, joy/thorns. In a rune reading, all of these appear together; only their positions vary according to where they land upon the cloth. Where they land will offer clues as to how they may be more harmoniously integrated into our daily lives.

STONES AND DIVINATION

Stone lends itself well to use as an oracle because it is of the Earth herself. Stones have been forming their shapes for millions of years. It is said that earth currents, captured in the vibration of the stones, stimulate the feminine-intuitive or right side of the brain.

Early peoples thought they detected signs, omens and oracles from the gods almost everywhere: in the clouds, in the stars, in the actions of animals and even in the markings on stones, which may help explain the origin of the runes. Such messages are still sent to us by these methods today, if only we have eyes to see them, as the following story demonstrates.

Some years ago, I met a young man who carried a stone in his pocket. This stone was roughly two inches square and about three-quarters of an inch thick. It was greenish-black in color and had many facets. While it was a totally natural piece of rock, this was no ordinary stone. When held at an oblique angle, the light caught the facets in a particular way and an almost photographic image of what looked like a Greek Orthodox priest, complete with hat and beard, appeared to be etched into it. Yet when one examined the stone by looking directly at it, the image was hardly visible. Amazed, I asked if there was a story connected with the stone, and this is what he told me:

The year before, while traveling through Europe, he met a young woman in France with whom he became quite enamored. They traveled through Greece together and lingered there for several weeks. Then she decided to go to Germany. My young friend, who remained in Greece a few days, was preparing to join her when suddenly he received a telegram from his brother in Spain. The brother's money had been stolen and he needed assistance. Needless to say, the young man felt torn. Should he go to Germany and be with his girlfriend, or rush to help his brother in Spain?

Later, while walking idly down a road, he walked past this particular stone and, as the light hit it in that certain way, he saw the image. Without thinking much about the matter, he picked up the stone and put it in his pocket. A day or so after this incident, still feeling quite depressed and very much torn, he saw a priest walking toward him down the street. As they drew closer to each other, my friend discovered, much to his surprise, that the priest looked very much like the image on the stone. The priest crossed the road, and when he was directly in front of the young man, stopped, looked into his eyes, said, "Follow your heart," and walked on. And so he did.

THE RUNES AND SELF-KNOWLEDGE

We often have helpers in life to show us where we are out of step on our path. These helpers may be good friends, therapists, teachers and/or healers. But there are times when no one is available; at these moments, it is both useful and comforting to turn to the runes for advice and counsel. Using the runes as a tool for self-knowledge is a lot like the young man being confronted by the Greek priest. The priest was able to look directly into the man's soul and tell him what he needed to hear at that very moment. The runes, if used correctly, will tell the truth about the heart and soul.

THE RUNES AND HEALING

Healing is wholeness, health and surrendering to that which is positive. Healing is being receptive to growth and change. Because the runes are by definition positive, they help to create a domain where one lives with positive options.

Maintaining a positive attitude toward self and the world promotes well-being in body, mind and spirit. We need to consciously focus on the process of healing because we live within a context where two simultaneous processes are occurring: evolution and entropy.

Evolution is life's natural tendency to progress, grow and transform. Entropy is a constant breaking-down process at work on all levels of life and all levels of the universe. In Hindu mythology, entropy is represented by the goddess Kali, the goddess of destruction; Skadi, the Teutonic and Scandinavian goddess of destruction, represents entropy in those cultures. In our bodies, our old cells are constantly breaking down and sloughing off while at the same time, new cells are being formed. Jung recognized this paradox and spent his whole life struggling with it. Its complete realization may be said to lie near the heart of Zen.

Healing, then, does not involve halting entropy or engaging in a vain attempt to stay alive by racing against time—both of which are impossible. Instead, it involves our becoming at ease with the entire process within our lives. Illness may manifest in the body, but lives in the mind. Therefore, all healing must take place in the mind, as well as the body. The runes heal by helping us to focus attention on positive rather than negative outcomes. When we keep choosing the positive, we create miracles.

THE RUNE MAGIC SYSTEM

Rune Magic, as a system of rune casting and divination, is based on the original *Anglo-Saxon Runic Poem*, one of the early runic manuscripts to survive a disastrous fire in Eighteenth-century England. The definitions are set in the same form of runic poetry as the original verses. The interpretations and techniques that follow are the result of years of personal study and practice with the runes.

The uniqueness of Rune Magic is that it is designed to be a wholly positive method of divination. Within this system of twenty-seven runic definitions, only two of the runes have negative connotations: (þ) the *Thorn*, and (ᚾ) *Nyd*, which could mean conflict or constraint. Between them, these symbols cover all the negative elements in life, and even these have positive aspects to them.

In Robert Muller's book, *New Genesis*, Pam Robbins is quoted as saying, "Optimism is more than an inherent disposition; it is an obligation, a responsibility." Robert Muller, Assistant Secretary General of the United Nations, says, "In order to model a happy and beautiful world, we must believe in it, we must work at it, we must be in love with it."

It is not my intent to deny the negative aspects of life, but rather to emphasize the positive wherever possible. *Rune Magic*, then, offers a positive context for learning an ancient system of wisdom from the viewpoint of optimism and faith.

The simplest method of using the runes is to cast them onto a cloth specially marked with three concentric circles, interpreting the patterns into which the runestones fall and noting the significance of the various circles in which they land. Small stones, coins, or pieces of wood inscribed with the twenty-seven runic symbols can be used. Usually they are read from the center of the cloth outward.

You can also use eleven stones, or any one of the special patterns described in the last chapter of the book, for a more structured reading. Or just a few runes can be pulled from the pouch at random and interpreted. In a very short time, you can learn to use the runes as shown in *Rune Magic* for yourself, your family and your friends.

THE RUNES AND SYNCHRONICITY

The runes, as well as all other oracles and systems of divination, work because of the phenomenon of "synchronicity." Synchronicity is one of those paradoxical concepts that even Webster's newest unabridged dictionary does not adequately define. It defines "synchronous" as "two or more events happening at the same moment in time." This definition does not take into account the "meaningful coincidence" and "interdependence of objective events" that pioneer psychological researcher Carl Jung talked about in his definition. Jung was interested in the phenomenon of synchronicity and delved into the *I-Ching*, the Tarot, numerology and astrology.

Jung defines synchronicity as

THE RUNES: AN ANCIENT ORACLE OF SELF-KNOWLEDGE

A concept that formulates a point of view diametrically opposed to that of causality . . . whereas synchronicity takes the coincidence of events in space and time as meaning something more than mere chance, namely, a peculiar inter-dependence of objective events among themselves, as well as with the subjective (psychic) states of the observer or observers.

By using a random casting method within a positive context that gives each stone an equal chance of landing in any one of the three circles, Rune Magic allows for maximum synchronicity. The more synchronicity in an already positive system, the more enlightening the reading. Trusting the runes to fall in such a way as to give an accurate picture of one's present state of awareness is to trust the Highest Source as an oracle. My daughter says that "synchronicity is God's way of saying 'Hi' to us!" If only as a reminder that there is One who *can* say "Hi" to us, synchronicity is a very useful concept.

THE RUNES AND CARL JUNG

For Jung, the fundamental psychological task facing all human beings is learning to become aware of the opposing states of being manifesting in our personality, often in the subconscious, and then by bringing them to conscious awareness, to synthesize and unify them into a harmonious working whole. As part of this process, Jung felt it was important to become conscious of the archetypal forces at work in our psyches. Archetypes, according to Jung, can be thought of as the basic building blocks of personality. They are personified characteristics, often opposites, that represent sections of the personality. These include the "shadow-side," the personifications of our negative traits, fears, anxieties or wishes.

Also of profound importance in Jungian thought is the concept of the *anima* and *animus*. The anima represents the feminine personality or energy within the male. The animus represents the masculine personality or energy within the female. Usually we project an idealized version of these qualities onto our mates and lovers. The trouble begins when we discover that the "real" person is not our idealized projection and also has a negative side. When this happens we sometimes act out these negative qualities ourselves, and sometimes provoke our mate into acting them out for us.

Important archetypes which can be found in the runes include: (ᛝ) *Ing*, the hero; (ᛦ) *Peordh*, the fool, the child or the *Puer Aeternis*; (ᚨ) *Aesc*, transformation; (ᛉ) *Ac*, the oak tree of free will or autonomy; (ᚹ) *Wynn*, joy; (ᚲ) *Cen*, knowledge or Logos; (ᛚ) *Lagu*, love or Eros; (ᚻ) *Haegl*, which can symbolize sexuality; (ᛇ) *Eoh*, the masculine energy; and (ᛒ) *Beorc*, the feminine energy, these last two representing the animus and the anima respectively.

Some of the archetypes among the runes which can reflect our shadow-sides are (ᚦ) the *Thorn* and (ᚾ) *Nyd*, which can mean conflict. When (ᛁ) *Is* is face-up it means clarity, intuition, the self; when face-down it may mean "not seeing," or "Nazi," of which there is one in each subconscious. Russell Schweikert, the first astronaut to catch a glimpse of our Earth as Gaia, made the statement, "The eye that does not see does not do justice to the body." The "I" that does not know its own divinity does not do justice to the soul.

In his introduction to Gail Fairfield's *Choice Centered Tarot*, Ralph Metzner, Professor of East-West Psychology at the California Institute of Integral Studies, acknowledges that from the Jungian point of view, "the Tarot . . . the *I Ching*, numerology, astrology, rune casting . . . and others [are devices] for not only predicting the future, but also for providing insight and symbolic tools for self-understanding . . . one would say that in a . . . reading there is a 'meaningful coincidence,' or synchronicity, between the symbols . . . and the person's life situation.''

It's a curious fact that Jung, who wrote so extensively about other oracular systems like the *I-Ching*, astrology and the Tarot, had little to say about the runes. Yet the runes, being a European system, were a part of his own heritage. It is obvious that Jung was familiar with the runes, as he once referred to the story of Odin hanging on the Yggdrasil. But strangely enough he only mentioned the runes themselves rather inconsequentially in a footnote: ''Hanging on the Tree of Life, Odin obtained knowledge of the runes and of the inspiriting drink that gave him immortality.'' And when Jung quoted the poem ''Havamel,'' he left out the last lines which tell of Odin's gaining the runes: ''I know that I hung/ On the windy tree/ all of the nights nine,/ wounded by spear/ and given to Odhinn,/ myself to myself,/ on that tree/ which no man knows/ from what roots it rises . . .''

At first it seems strange that Jung omitted the last lines of this poem. One would think that Jung would have included the part in which Odin finally discovers what he has been seeking. The answer to this curious paradox lies in the very mysterious, complex, negative role that the runes played in Germany during Jung's time. According to Dr. Johannes Stein, a professor of modern history who was both a personal acquaintance of the youthful Adolph Hitler and later an advisor to Winston Churchill on Hitler, the dictator, who was interested in darker forms of the occult, used the runes to strengthen his own black power. In fact, in Germany the runes had a long history as a lower form of magic. Teutonic women of the poorer classes were paid to cast spells for purposes as diverse as murder and romance.

There is at least one passage supporting this theory in which Jung refers to the way the temper of the times leads even a scholar into the grips of an almost overpowering frenzy and obsession:

> Haver himself is *ergriffen* by the depths of meaning in the primal words lying at the root of the Germanic languages, to an extent that he certainly never knew before. Haver, the Indologist, is not to blame for this, nor yet the *Edda*; it is rather the fault of *Kairos*, the present moment in time— whose name on closer investigation turns out to be Wotan.

The "primal words" which Jung refers to are either the runes themselves or early Scandinavian words written in a runic language. Such runic words, which were supposed to possess mystical or primal potency, were becoming the rage among Hitler's followers and those who idealized Nietzsche (represented by Wotan).

One could speculate why Jung chose not to give importance to the runes, nor to finish the poem describing Odin's acquiring them. Jung did not leave off those last six lines of "Havamel" because he did not *know* of the runes. Jung's deep interest in mysticism would naturally have led him into exploring the runic symbols. For Jung to write about the runes would have been to feed into the fanaticism of his time. In his silence, he showed respect for their ancient wisdom. With the darkness of those particular years behind us, a path has been cleared for bringing forth the runes once again as an oracle of light.

BLACK AND WHITE MAGIC

It is important when using any kind of oracle to know the difference between "black" and "white" magic. If we use an oracle to "cast a spell" on someone, or to manipulate or wish them harm, this is obviously "black magic." The real difference between black and white magic, however, is whether the person using the runes has faced the darkness, or shadow-side, within themself. The shadow side is that aspect of a person which has not yet been made conscious. By consciously embracing one's shadow-side, one will be given the strength to clarify and reflect the light in the self and others. Those who face the darkness in themselves and expose it to the light can then use the runes and remain free from harm.

Many people who practice divination are sensitive about having their oracle handled by a potential client, for fear of having it contaminated by the other's vibrations. While this is a reasonable attitude, some people can also use it as a way of exerting power over a client. This is not black magic but could be considered a form of "gray magic." At best, we must be wary of diviners who say that *only they* have the answers to how the runes or any oracle are to be used.

Using the rune system as offered in this book, you always invite your client to handle the runestones and cast them on the cloth. The rune-reader is only an interpreter of the reading. Rune Magic, then, used as described in this book, is a system of "white magic."

CHAPTER II

HISTORY OF THE RUNES

Ask and it shall be given unto you;
Given unto you, it shall give you
trouble; Through trouble, you will
know God.
—St. John, from *The Essene Gospel*

THE CELTS AND THE VIKINGS

The actual history of the runes may be as convoluted as
the interweavings of Celtic knots, and much of what we do
know about them is subject to conjecture. For many centuries the runes were used by the ancient Indo-European
pagan tribes in Scandinavia and Great Britain—and later by
the Vikings and Germans as an oral system of divination,
steeped in mystery and magic. It is quite possible, however,
that the history of the runes goes back to the beginning of
mankind's time here on Earth. Perhaps all languages started
out as sacred oracular systems first used by priests and
priestesses who had been initiated in the ancient temples.
We know that not only the runes but Chinese, Sanskrit,
Hebrew and certain Celtic systems began this way.

The Celts also seem to have used a system of divination
based on casting and interpreting patterns of lines or characters, usually carved into stone, wood or bone, called
Ogham, or *Ogam*, probably named for the Celtic god of eloquence. He was sometimes equated with Hercules because
the Celts believed that eloquence was more powerful than

Table of Historical Definitions

ANGLO-SAXONS: The Angles and Saxons were pagan tribes from Germany who, along with the Jutes (from Denmark), invaded England after the Romans of the fifth century A.D.

BARBARIANS: From the Greek word *barbaros*, meaning bearded. "Barbarian" refers to the Indo-European peoples who lived rurally and wore beards, such as the Celtic tribes who traveled to Greece and Rome.

CELTS (KELTS): Tribes of Indo-European rural people sharing a common linguistic origin. They originated from the Baltic countries and Scandinavia, traveled across and populated much of rural Europe from 3000 B.C. to at least the first century A.D., and eventually settled in Northern France and the British Isles, where remnants of their culture still remain. They worshipped pagan gods and nature. Their priests and priestesses were the Druids.

DRUIDS: The priests, priestesses, shamans and seers of the Celtic tribes. "Druid" means "being close to the oak" and "thrice wise." They worshipped nature deities in circles of oak groves. They were bards—poets and musicians. They were well versed in astronomy and astrology and led all rituals and sacrifices. They presided over the week-long tribal councils held at least once a year to decide tribal laws.

HEATHENS: A sixteenth-century name given by the Catholics which referred to the Scots in Northern England who lived on hills. "Heath" means hill. The term later became a slang word to mean all non-Christian peoples.

INDO-EUROPEANS: All those people sharing a common system of linguistics and culture who made up the ancestry of the British Isles. The Celts were Indo-European but the Romans were not.

PAGANS: Indo-European tribes who worshipped nature deities, tree spirits and pantheons of gods and goddesses.

VIKINGS: Tribes of Indo-European travelers, mostly from Scandinavian countries, who built elaborate boats and explored Europe's waterways. "Viking" was originally a verb and meant to go adventuring and exploring ("to go-a-viking"). They worshipped pagan gods, as did the Celts, and traveled Europe's waterways. They flourished from the sixth to the twelfth centuries A.D.

strength. Traces of Ogham, along with runes, were found carved into stone monuments and crosses throughout Ireland, Scotland and Northern England long before the Vikings arrived there. Runes are also found carved into monuments and sites sacred to the old pagan cultures all over Scandinavia and the British Isles.

According to one school of thought, the runes originated with the Etruscans, an ancient people who around 1300 B.C. migrated by sea from the Steppes of Asia Minor into a portion of Northern Italy called Etruria. According to the *Encyclopedia Britannica*, the Etruscans were artisans, dancers and metalcrafters. The characters of their language somewhat resemble early Greek or Roman letters—but also because of their linear design, resemble runes. For this reason, many scholars believe the Etruscans may have also originated the runes. Another fact which suggests this connection is that portions of Etruria later became Umbria in Italy, and the seat of Anglo-Saxon runic learning in Ireland is Northumbria. The Etruscan culture disappeared mysteriously several hundred years before the advent of the Romans, leaving little more than their graves as evidence for scholars.

Runes are popularly associated with the Vikings and the sagas of Norse mythology and with Odin, the god of the runes. In their magnificent boats, the Vikings traveled all over Europe's waterways and across much of its land as well. In their wake they left behind boats, amulets and many large stone monoliths elaborately carved and decorated with runes. Although the runes are identified with the Norse, who created myths and sagas around them, they apparently were not their originators.

At least three thousand years before the Vikings set forth in their beautiful long boats, an earlier Indo-European people traveled and traded throughout Europe, the British Isles and into Asia. Though the people who descended from these roots became the Celts, the Scythians, the Vikings and other barbarian tribes who migrated and settled throughout Europe, they shared a common origin: the Kurgan tribe, which originally lived somewhere around Lithuania.

The Celtic and Viking cultures fluctuated back and forth across Europe in a single continuous migration covering three millennia. One of their similarities is their use of twisted, braided knotwork with which they decorated everything. Both the Celts and the Vikings were pagan and worshipped nature deities, and tree spirits. Both cultures have matriarchal roots and the Celts gave equal power to women. Both cultures shared a calendar whose day began at sundown rather than sunrise, like the Jewish system. In fact, the main difference between these two cultures was the Druids, who were found among the Celts but not among the Vikings.

THE DE DANANNS AND THE FOMORIANS

According to Legend, in 2000 B.C. a pre-Celtic tribe from the area of the Baltic migrated by boat to Ireland. They were known as the *De Dananns*, or *Tuatha De Danann*, "the Children of the Goddess Danu." These people were fine stone-carvers and metalcraftspeople and were the first to bring music to Ireland. Long before the *De Dananns* arrived, a group of tall and mighty warriors called the Fomorians inhabited Ireland. Several battles were fought in which the *De Dananns* usurped power from the Fomorians.

One Irish legend dating from this period reveals the power which the ancient Celts attributed to the runic language: Dagda was one of the Druid bards and spiritual leaders of the *De Danann* tribe. In the famous battle of *Mag Tured*, the Fomorians carried off Dagda's harp. Thinking they had eluded their pursuers, the Fomorians gathered in their dining hall and prepared a feast with Dagda's harp hanging on the wall as a trophy. Just as they had all sat down, the *De Dananns* burst into the hall. Dagda called to his harp, and the harp is said to have spirited itself off the wall and into Dagda's hands again. Dagda sang three short songs before he left. The first was a plaintive tune which made all the women cry. The second was a song of mirth which made all the men laugh. The third was a lullaby which put everyone to sleep, and the *De Dananns* safely returned to their own camp with the harp.

Although the *De Dananns* were fine stone carvers and worshipped in the great circles of standing stones called *cromlechs*, the Celts were probably not the ones who erected these mysterious sites. The growth of peat over some of these stone circles indicates that they were put in place long before the arrival of the *De Dananns*. The Fomorians were also workers in stone and are believed to have been the ones who built these stone circles, not only throughout Ireland, but possibly in other parts of Western Europe as well.

Some students of the runes have come to believe that the Fomorians were descendants of Atlantis and that the runes were first used on this ancient continent before the last great consciousness-closing. Perhaps this is why the runes appear on the wall of the inner temple at Newgrange, as Danaan Parry notes in his Introduction.

Following the *De Dananns*, another pre-Celtic tribe, the Milesians, or "Sons of Milid," invaded Ireland. The Milesians, who eventually defeated the *De Dananns*, introduced agriculture to Ireland, as well as the *Brehon Laws*, which constitute the basic Celtic laws of commerce and payment of debts and fines. Fines were to be paid in cattle, an early form of money. It is interesting to note that the first two runic symbols in the Anglo-Saxon *Futhorc* are *Feoh* (ᚠ), meaning money or prosperity, and *Ur* (ᚢ), meaning oxen or cattle. Can this be purely coincidental?

Although the Celtic tribes traveled throughout Europe for two thousand years before Christ, their first real homeland was in Gaul, in the area near where Chartres Cathedral stands today. They lived tribally on farmsteads throughout Europe and once a year came together for tribal council meetings led by the Druids. Among the Celts' many gifts to civilization were their ironworks—they perfected the iron-spoked wagon wheel and invented chain-metal armor—the plowshare, crop rotation and an improved flour mill. They also introduced soap to the Greeks and Romans. The Celts achieved their greatest period of influence in the last six hundred years B.C. In 390 B.C. the Celts invaded Republican Rome, and in 279 B.C., pillaged Delphi in Greece.

THE ROMANS AND THE CHRISTIANS

Between 58 and 51 B.C., Julius Caesar and his armies conquered Gaul and pushed the Celtic tribes back into Britain, marking the beginning of the Roman Empire, but not the end of the Celtic one.

Celtic culture and language continued to flourish in the British Isles despite many invasions by the Romans and Germans. Since their spiritual tradition was oral, it could not be destroyed. In Ireland, Tara, a most sacred spot since the time of the Fomorians and Milesians, became the new homeland of the Celts and the place where the tribal council meetings were held after the defeat of Gaul. In 433 A.D. Tara became the site of one of the first Christian monasteries founded by St. Patrick.

Although it seems as if a peaceful crossover from the pagan to the Christian religion took place in Ireland, this may only be true from the Christian viewpoint. With the advent of Christianity, the runes, along with the Druids and all the old pagan religions that gave the Goddess equal place in their worship, were considered to be of the Devil and through neglect and persecution fell into disuse and obscurity.

As a result, the oldest document in a runic language known to exist is the *Poetic Eddas*, which came to us from the Vikings, the last holdout against Christianity in Europe. The *Eddas* were written by a group of Vikings, who settled in Iceland to escape the oppression of their king. They wrote them to celebrate their Viking lineage and to set down permanently the classic sagas of Norse legend. Together they also created one of the first European democratic governments, called the *Allthing*—and Odin was often called the *Allfather*.

A book published in 1474, called *Saxon Northumbrian Pagan Runes*, says that the runes were in existence since at least 54 A.D., and from 54 to 630 A.D. the order was under the pagan god "Noden," obviously one of the names of Odin. But there is little resemblance between these early runes and the ones that originated in the *Anglo-Saxon Runic Poem*, on which the runes in this book are based.

If the history of the runes still seems a mystery, perhaps it should remain that way. That their roots go deeper into time than our present historians can trace does not diminish their significance, but rather supports their wisdom. The runes are a gift of the Spirit, the stepping stones of our timeless journey home.

CHAPTER III

MYTH AND THE RUNES

The real mystery [of the Kabbalah] is how we let the obvious become so hidden. —Martin Buber

IDUN'S APPLES

Mythology is the history of our belief systems, of the stories we have created in an attempt to explain or approach the Divine. The runes are one of those tools rooted in ancient mythology that have high practicality in our changing contemporary lives. Understanding some of their history and mythology helps us to get a grasp on how they were once used and how they can best be used now.

According to legend, Odin was the chief of the Norse Gods and the creator of the runes. He was Hermes in Greek mythology, Mercury in Roman mythology and is said to have come to Egypt from Atlantis. Odin was also Logos, the god of communication, healing and the occult. All the gods and goddesses lived in Yggdrasil, the tree of life, death and transformation. Yggdrasil was far more than a tree; it was the domain of the entire Norse cosmolgoy. Yggdrasil had three levels, and each level was made up of three regions.

At its root were the three regions of the Underworld. One was Hel, the land of the dead. The second was the land of the Giants, where Odin was born and, with the goddess Frigg, sired many of the other gods and goddesses. The third realm was the land of the Dark Elves.

The second level of Yggdrasil was Midgard, or Middle Earth, where the mortals lived; it contained oceans and mountains and deserts. Midgard was surrounded by a giant serpent who constantly gnawed at Yggdrasil's roots and branches. In another region lived the three Norns, who represented the three phases of the moon: waxing, full and waning. They also symbolized the psyche and/or the Great Mother. It was they who watered and nurtured Yggdrasil daily, ensuring its growth. Also at this level was the Fountain of Mimir, or Well of Wisdom. Many animals, such as goats and birds, lived on and about Yggdrasil. A squirrel (the ego) continually ran up and down the tree trunk, trying to make discord between the snake of the Underworld (our lower self) and the eagle perched aloft in Asgard (our higher self).

At the top level of Yggdrasil, the branches formed Asgard, where Odin and the other gods and goddesses, called Aesir, dwelled. Here was found Valhalla, the sacred temple of the gods, whose walls were made of gold and whose ceiling was lined with crossed swords. Valhalla had over five hundred doors which were opened to allow the entrance of the mortal heroes who had died in battle.

According to some Norse legends, the runes did not originate with Odin but were attributed to the Norse goddess Idun, or Iduna, the feminine counterpart to Odin. Like Olwen in Celtic mythology and Hera in Greek mythology, Idun nurtured and sustained the gods with the golden apples of immortality that she grew in her garden.

In the retelling of the classic myth, "The Theft of Idun's Apples," by Kevin Crossly-Holland, Odin and two other gods, Honir and Loki, were exploring another part of Midgard when an evil giant, disguised as an eagle, dragged away Honir and threatened to kill him. As a ransom for Honir, the eagle asked for Idun's apples. Loki ("the changing one") donned Freyja's falcon skin and flew to the castle where Idun lived. The eagle followed Loki to Idun's castle. When Loki saw the eagle hovering, he changed Idun into a hazelnut and held her in his mouth. Apparently Loki was gone for so long getting Idun and her apples that all the gods began to wither and grow old like mortals. When Loki finally returned as a falcon with nothing but a hazelnut, everyone was worried that he had forsaken them by not bringing Idun back to them. The myth goes on to say:

> Loki threw off Freyja's falcon skin. He looked at the grey, anxious ones pressing around him and scornfully laughed in their faces. Then the Sky Traveller bent over his trophy (the nut); he cradled it between his hands and softly spoke the runes. Idun stood there, young and supple and smiling. She moved innocent among the ailing gods. She offered them apples.

The gods were once again restored to health and immortality. Idun's consort, Bragi, became the greatest of the bards because she engraved the magic runes into his tongue. Our English word "brag" probably comes from Bragi. This is what has led some scholars to speculate that Idun's apples may have been the runes.

It is said that Odin wanted to find the runes in order to discover the secret of Idun's immortality, or his feminine self. First Odin drank from Mimir, the Fountain of Wisdom, and then hung (perhaps upside down) on the Yggdrasil, the Ash Tree of Transformation, without food or drink for nine days and nights to learn the runes.

The poem "Havamel," from the *Poetic Edda*, reads as follows:

> I know that I hung
> On the windy tree
> All of the nights nine,

> wounded by spear
> and given to Odhinn,
> myself to myself,
> On that tree, which no man knows,
> from what roots it rises.
> They dealt me no bread
> nor drinking horn,
> I looked down, I took up the runes
> I took them screaming,
> I fell back from there.

This sounds very much like a self-imposed initiation, for hanging upside down was one of the many initiatory rites practiced by the people of those times to "cleanse the doors of perception."

The significance of these voluntary ordeals can best be explained by the famous Zen story about the student who went to his Master and asked to know the meaning of Zen or life. The student was soon busy explaining his own views on Zen. The Master invited the student to stay for tea. The student held forth his cup, and the Master poured tea into it from the teapot. Even after the cup was full, the Master kept pouring and the tea soon overran the cup and saucer and spilled onto the floor. The Master continued to pour. Finally, unable to keep still any longer, the student asked the Master why he continued to pour the tea. The Master replied: "Your own cup is already full. You have no room for further knowledge until it is emptied."

LEFT BRAIN, RIGHT BRAIN

Odin's ordeal or initiation represents the period it took him to empty his logical left brain (or masculine self) and bring his intuitive right brain (feminine self) to bear in interpreting or understanding the symbolic runes. At the crossover point, when both sides of the brain achieved balance, Odin understood the runes and all of life in its entirety.

In *Jung and Tarot*, Sallie Nichols echoes this idea, explaining the significance of the "Hanged Man," one of the Tarot cards, in terms of the physical sensations being suspended in this ritual posture produces:

> Then we would feel how the blood rushes to our head, bringing oxygen to the brain and reviving our spirit. Our jaded retinas would be revived, suffusing our view of the world with fresh color. If, like the Hanged Man, we were suspended in this posture, alone and without food or companionship, our "doors of perception" would be so cleansed that we might experience heavenly visions and the illumination of satori.

Odin may have been the original "Hanged Man"—the first to undergo this cleansing ritual during those nights and days he hung suspended between the two worlds of darkness and light; of the masculine (assertive) and the feminine (receptive); of the conscious and the unconscious; of knowledge and intuition. It is said that Odin lost his left eye as he hung on Yggdrasil, putting it out with his own sword as part of his efforts to gain the apples of Idun. Odin symbolically removed the hindrance of his left eye—giving him limited perception and perhaps more access to his right brain.

Although Odin lost one eye, he gained the "Whole of Life," a new viewpoint engraved forever on his soul. He found the runes and a way of translating them into life as a gift for humanity, providing a means to acquire knowledge and produce personal transformation.

The runes, like Idun's apples, come from the feminine, intuitive, feeling aspect of ourselves, the right brain. But understanding the meaning of them and communicating to others also requires the use of the cognitive, thinking, masculine aspect of the left brain. Thus the necessity of bringing the two into balance or equilibrium.

The runic verse for the symbol that represents the masculine energy is (ᛇ) *Eoh*, the yew tree. It says, "A tree with rough bark, hardy and firm in the earth, supported by its roots, the guardian of the flame, keeper of the estate." This aspect of ourselves, while rooted in the earth (or our feminine selves), suggests a responsible, conservational attitude that we traditionally ascribe to the masculine. Its purpose is to deal with the manipulations necessary for survival on the physical plane.

The symbol that represents the feminine energy is (ᛒ) *Beorc*, the poplar tree. The runic verse which describes this tree says, "The bough with the greenest of leaves. It has no fruit or flowers, yet without seeds it produces shoots. It is glorious in its branches, tall in its crown, fairly adorned, heavy with leaves, reaching to the sky." Although this symbol suggests a barren female, it produces shoots and is fertile nonetheless. This type of energy, like the masculine, also comes from the earth, but it reaches up toward Heaven.

If we think of masculine energy as horizontal, oriented toward the physical plane, and feminine energy as vertical, oriented toward a higher plane, then the intersection of the two produces a cross. the rune (ᚷ) *Gyfu*, which is a diagonal cross, not only means relationship, but also signifies giving. If the point where the two lines meet, the blending of the masculine and feminine, can represent the heart, then this could provide the key to a profound new mythology for the Aquarian Age.

Druid mythology has taught us to honor and respect the Earth and Nature. Jewish philosophy has taught us that there is only one God and that God is everywhere. The Christian era has taught us that each of us is created in

God's image. The mythology of the Aquarian Age reminds us that we are not only created in God's image, we *are* God, because God and God's creations are inseparable. And with that knowledge comes the responsibility to love, cherish and respect all life.

Is it any surprise the runes have reemerged at the crossroads of our time to remind us that wholeness and health, both as individuals and as a living planet, are always the result of acknowledging and embracing both the masculine and feminine in ourselves, and that the whole is more than the sum of its separate parts.

CHAPTER IV

THE FUTHORC: THE RUNES AND THEIR MEANINGS

The *Futhorc* is the name of the so-called alphabet of the runes. It is an acronym of the first six runic characters. There are as many different Futhorcs as there are alphabets: there is the Norse *Futhorc*, the German *Futhorc*, the Anglo-Saxon *Futhorc* and the Icelandic *Futhorc*. Each one varies according to its origin. The *Futhorc* used in *Rune Magic* is based on the Anglo-Saxon or Celtic system, with some slight variations.

In the *Anglo-Saxon Runic Poem*, two more runes were given than are used in this book: after (ᚫ) *Aesc* in the standard system, is the rune (ᛠ) *Yr*, which means a war-tool or amulet used as a weapon; and (ᛠ) *Ear*, meaning death, or a dead body. Since *Aesc* (ash) already means transformation and returning to the Earth, I have deliberately omitted these last two runes.

In addition I have taken the liberty of changing the accepted definition of (ᛇ) *Eoh*, the yew tree. The Anglo-Saxon verse for *Eoh* reads: "A tree with rough bark, hardy and firm in the earth, supported by its roots, the guardian of the flame, keeper of the estate." To me this seems like a perfect description of the masculine energy. Other scholars

The FUTHORC
(The Runic Alphabet)

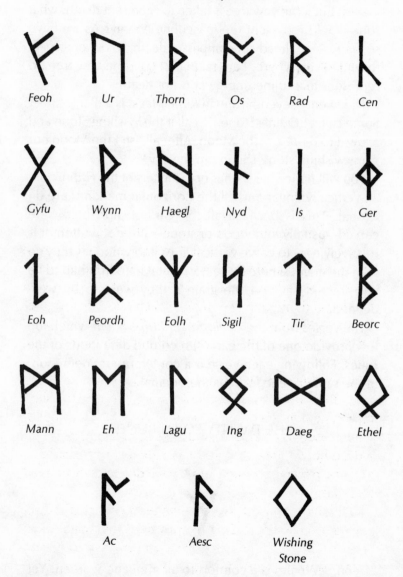

Feoh	Ur	Thorn	Os	Rad	Cen
Gyfu	Wynn	Haegl	Nyd	Is	Ger
Eoh	Peordh	Eolh	Sigil	Tir	Beorc
Mann	Eh	Lagu	Ing	Daeg	Ethel
Ac	Aesc	Wishing Stone			

FIGURE 1

29

have suggested that the yew tree really represents death or the Underworld, as it was once traditionally planted on graves. But if the yew tree is taken to represent death, what rune would represent the masculine energy? As we have seen, (ᚫ) *Aesc* already encompasses death, so out of respect for men everywhere, I am taking (ᛇ) *Eoh*, the yew tree, to represent masculine energy and not death.

The twenty-seventh rune in *Rune Magic* is a blank stone. Some call it "Odin's Stone." I call it the Wishing Stone and allow it to represent the Moon. After all, isn't the Moon our giant wishing stone shining in the sky?

You will notice the shapes of the letters of the *Futhorc* are all vertically linear and all the horizontal markings are diagonal. This is because all the earliest alphabets were carved—usually into wood or stone—and not written. It is relatively easy to carve vertical lines into wood, as they go with the grain, whereas the horizontal markings had to be cut precisely against the grain if they were to be well-defined.

The verses from the *Anglo-Saxon Runic Poem* which follow provide one of the earliest recorded definitions of the runes. Following each verse is a contemporary definition, in the same poetic form as the original.

THE TWENTY-SEVEN RUNES

Feoh: "Wealth is a comfort to all men and women. Yet everyone must give it away freely if he wants to gain glory in the Lord's sight." Wealth and prosperity are not measured by how much we have but by how much we have to share.

Prosperity is an attitude: we can have millions and feel poor, or we can share the little we have with others and feel like a million. Prosperity defined as sharing with others implies a culture which respects community, since we cannot be truly wealthy and live in isolation. Can there truly be such a thing as a prosperous miser? *Key phrases:* abundance, plenty, prosperity, wealth, having enough to share.

Ur (ox, strength, physical power): "The ox, a savage beast, is fierce and has huge horns. A great roamer of the moorlands, it fights with its horns. It is a courageous brute." The physical body. The life-force energy. Strength, physical power. Any power which must be tamed.

When the *Futhorc* was first compiled, *Ur*, the ox, meant the beast, or the external forces of nature with which people had to contend. Over time, the nature of the beast was changed. Now the forces with which we must contend are our own ego, our physical body, our health, our psychospiritual self. The external forces of nature we must contend with now include nuclear power. *Key phrases:* the physical body, the ego, health, that which needs taming in ourselves and others, the planet as a whole.

Thorn: "The thorn is extremely sharp. Grabbing hold of it is painful to any warrior, uncommonly severe to anyone who lies among them." In life there are roses and roses have thorns. Being aware of the thorns is our key to understanding them. Our problems are creative opportunities. Our fears, challenges.

The thorns imply any actions or nonactions through which we can get stuck. As humans, we get stuck when we react to another person's feelings or actions (or our own) and take them too seriously. *Thorn* can mean the barriers on our path, and/or can also be the creative opportunities which come from solving these problems. Thorns can be a barrier or a needed kick in the pants. *Key phrases:* thorns, barriers, stumbling blocks, problems to be dealt with, creative opportunities.

Os (the mouth): "The mouth—origin of all speech, the prop of wisdom and the comfort of the wise and a joy and consolation to every man." Communication was highly valued by the Druids and the Vikings, as was respect for the word and for wisdom. Communication is the most precious tool in the universe, our key to planetary survival.

In these times, we all recognize the importance of communicating our basic ideas and common values. This may be done with language and more intuitively, with our feelings. Even if we cannot understand another's language, we can still feel another's emotional state. *Os* also means the mouth, perhaps the speaker. *Key phrases:* mouth, communication, speaker, speaking, opening.

Rad (travel): "In the hall *rad* is pleasant for every warrior, and very energetic for the man who sits on the back of a powerful horse covering the mile-long road." *Rad* not only means travel, but sudden changes in profession, location and spiritual direction.

Travel may also mean change. In astrology *Rad* may be somewhat like the energy of Uranus. *Rad* did not always designate a pleasure trip, since back in Viking and Druidic times, one encountered storms, hazardous weather and battles along the way. *Key phrases:* travel, changes, journeys, trips.

Cen (the torch): "*Cen* is known to all living things by its flame, pale and bright." The torch is the ever-present light guiding the path of the heart. Wherever it lights the way, we follow.

The torch is our guiding light. The Old English word *ken* means "to know." Therefore, *Cen* is the light which guides us on our path, but also the intelligence deep within us which guides our heart. *Cen*, the torch, is the truth; how we know what we know. It is the small voice within us. It is conscious awareness, the lamp of knowledge. *Key phrases:* the torch, truth, the light within, the inner voice, knowledge.

Gyfu (giving): "The act of giving, generosity. Generosity is a grace and an honor, a support and a glory, and a help and sustenance to any outcast who is deprived of it." Giving is the key to prosperity. When you do not feel prosperous, begin by sharing. When you do not feel you have enough to share, begin by forgiving.

Gyfu means being receptive to the gifts of others. As such it may also mean relationships, as it suggests give and take. *Key phrases:* generosity, giving, gratitude, relationship, lack of relationship and/or forgiveness (when facedown).

Wynn (joy): "Joyful is the person who knows no miseries, afflictions or sorrow and who has prosperity and happiness and the wealth of great towns." Joy is the bubble of enthusiasm and peace that surrounds us. Joy is the echo of God's life in us.

Our natural response to the experience of our aliveness

is joy. We are more inclined to feel joy from a deep space within, although the feeling of joy may be triggered in response to another. Joy, like laughter, is infectious. *Key phrases:* joy, laughter, merriment, deep satisfaction, contentment.

Haegl (snow): "The whitest of grains. It swirls from the heights of heaven and is tossed about in gusts of wind. Then it turns to water." The seeds of opportunity and abundance shower upon us like snow. What we have earned in the universe comes back to us tenfold.

Even in Viking days *Haegl (hail)* meant inclement weather. But it also represents a transient energy in constant flux, ephemeral in nature, not fixed. It may also mean karma, but not necessarily negative karma. It is definitely an external force. *Key phrases:* pleasure (including sexual pleasure), opportunities, catastrophes, a shower of gifts, bad weather.

Nyd: "Constraint, warning, need, oppression, affliction. Affliction constricts the heart, but it often serves as a help and salvation to the people if they attend to it in time." *Nyd* is our way of knowing where the thorns are so that we may stop and take heed in time. Also, a dispute, conflict or disagreement, as in law. When *Nyd* appears face-down, it means "don't worry"!

It can also mean conflict or lies, as well as sparring with words, as in litigation, or the kind of sport that was practiced in Shakespeare's time, as when Romeo's and Juliet's families sparred with each other in the streets. *Nyd* can mean differences of opinion, arguments. It can also mean paradox, which is a way of resolving conflicts when something is neither all white nor all black. *Key phrases:* conflict, constraints, arguments, paradoxes.

I

Is (pronounced *ice*): "The ice is very cold, extremely slippery. A floor, fair to the sight, made by the frost, glitters like jewels, clear as glass." "I," the eye, is our bridge from us to God. When the ice is like glass, we have become a mirror reflecting God. Intellect, intuition, integrity. "I" is knowing with the wisdom of the heart.

Whenever we utter the word "I" we are declaring ourselves to be one with our Higher God-Self. *Is* is also the eye that sees, our vision, seeing with the clarity of truth. When it is upside down, it is our inner vision. *Key phrases:* I, eye, Higher Truth, clarity, vision, to envision.

Ger (abundance): "A fruitful year is a boon to men and women. Fertility. A year of good harvest is a joy to people, when God, Holy King of Heaven, makes the earth give forth bright fruit for the rich and the poor." *Ger* means abundance, gestation, pregnancy, a time of fruition, bringing forth the harvest.

It is important to realize that while abundance may be the fruition and culmination of our work, like joy, it is already within us and surrounding us. *Ger* may also be the period of gestation. Coupled with *Ing*, the hero, *Ger* may also indicate the gestation of work or a project. *Ger* also indicates a binding commitment, as in marriage. *Key phrases:* Abundance, commitment, fulfillment, harvest, pregnancy, gestation.

Eoh (*Ih*) (yew tree): "A tree with rough bark, hardy and firm in the earth, supported by its roots, the guardian of the flame, keeper of the estate." The yew tree represents the masculine energy, grounded, responsible for the physical domain. It takes its nurturing and support from the earth.

In Scandinavian mythology, the yew tree represents Yggdrasil, the Tree of Life, and in Scandinavian countries the yew is often planted on graves to guard the dead. In the Anglo-Saxon translation of the Runes, *Eoh*, the yew tree, could also mean the masculine energy which manages and takes charge of things, assertiveness. *Key phrases:* management, to manage, masculine energy, to handle finances, keeper of the flame, master of the estate. (This energy is also present in females.)

Peordh (the fool, laughter, amusement): "A continual source of laughter and amusement for the great—where warriors sit cheerfully together in the beer hall." By knowing when not to take things too seriously, it is the wise fool who, through merriment and laughter, holds the whole picture together.

Peordh can be our own inner child, our children, our creativity, and/or our pets. It is a very important symbol in our times because it represents humor and whimsey. Life would not be complete without gaiety and lightness. *Key phrases:* humor, laughter, the fool, the child, pets, fun, whimsey.

Eolh (elk, protection, sanctuary): "Our Spirit Guides, our Protectors, our Guardian Angels shining their love upon us."

The Ancients knew that all of us have "Spirit Guides" or "Guardian Angels" watching over our lives and fortunes. *Key phrases:* Protectors, guardians, Spirit Guides.

Ꝩ

Sigil (Sun): "The Sun is a continual joy to seamen when they take a sea-steed over the fish's bath until it brings them to land." The Sun is our continuous benevolent source of light and life, radiating generous rays of warmth and well-being upon us all, rich and poor alike.

The Sun is our manifest Father, without whose warmth and energy we could not exist on our planet earth. Where *Sigil* falls in a reading, it amplifies, strengthens and illuminates what it is near. If it falls in the Center of Being, that person radiates Sun energy from their Center. *Key phrases:* Sun, warmth, light.

↑

Tir (the one-handed god, glory): "*Tir* is one of the guiding marks. It keeps the faith well towards princes and princesses. Above night's clouds it is always on its path and never fails. Guiding star." *Tir*, or glory, is the Star of Faith. Each of us has a star of our own shining forever in Heaven. "I shine for you on the darkest of nights and the cloudiest of days, therefore keep faith with me."

Tir is the Norse God who served Odin with such faith that he lost his hand and still remained loyal. *Tir* means faith, trust, being willing to take a risk. When *Tir* lands face-down, it means inner faith or lack of faith. *Key phrases:* glory, faith, star, loyalty, trust.

Beorc (birch or poplar tree): "The bough with the greenest of leaves. It has no fruit or flowers, yet without seeds it produces shoots. It is glorious in its branches, tall in its crown, fairly adorned, heavy with leaves reaching the sky." *Beorc* is the feminine energy. The poplar tree grows green and full and gives of itself just in being. She stands tall, yet firm to the earth, sways in the breeze and is glorious.

The poplar tree seems to lend its description to the female, or the Goddess energy, just as *Eoh* lends itself to the masculine energy. *Key phrases:* tree, feminine energy, green, giving.

Mann (man): "In his mirth, man is dear to his kinsmen. Yet each is bound to fail his fellow because the Lord, by His decree, wishes to commit the wretched body to the earth."

Mann means the people. People are immortal souls living in mortal bodies. Such is our precarious preciousness, the paradox of people. *Mann*, in this sense, takes in all of the human family. *Key phrases:* mankind, humanity, people, family.

Eh (horse): "The horse, the charger, proud of its hoofs, is a prince's delight in the presence of warriors, while rich men on horseback discuss its points. For the restless it is always a source of relaxation." The horse is a steadfast steed which provides both support and pleasure, mighty servant and loyal companion to man. Our vehicle of pleasure, work, and right-livelihood.

One may ask how the horse also serves as our work. A vehicle may be just that: a mode of extending ourselves in the world. *Eh* may also literally mean a vehicle, such as an automobile, boat, plane or RV. In the context of any reading, the definition chooses itself. *Key phrases:* horse, vehicle, "axe," means of transportation, our work.

Lagu (water): "Water seems interminable to men if they have to venture on the lolling ship and the sea waves scare them out of their wits, and the surf-horse does not respond to its bridle."

Our feelings, like the water, can be as turbulent as the stormy sea or as merry and playful as a bubbling brook. They may run the gamut, but basically there are really only two: love and fear. When turned face-down, *Lagu* may indicate inner feelings, or lack of self-esteem and self-love. *Key phrases:* feelings, emotions, love, the flow, "going with the flow," water.

Ing (the hero): "*Ing*, God of Fertility, who rides in the Chariot." *Ing* was the Scandinavian god of fertility and abundance. The hero is the human expressing divinity in his present life.

The hero can also be our own Higher Self. When we are being heroic, we attract the hero and we see the hero in others as well. In English, "ing," when added to a word, suggests any action, quality or state of being happening in the present. The hero may be our teacher, lover, and/or our most actualizing self. Perhaps *Ing*, the hero, also means one who is in the present. *Key phrases:* hero, beloved, teacher, Higher Self, being in the now.

Daeg (day): "The day, dear to men and women, is the Lord's gift, the Creator's glorious light. It is a joy and solace to rich and poor and of use to everyone!" Honor each day as it comes to you. For each day is God's new gift of creation, a chance for self-renewal and self-expression. Meditate.

This symbol gives us the opportunity to acknowledge each day and make it special. By focusing on life one day at a time, we create a fertile atmosphere for miracles. *Daeg* also means meditation as a conscious way of acknowledging each day. *Key phrases:* day, meditation, one day at a time.

Ethel (home or land): "Ancestral home, property. The ancestral home is dear to every man; in his house he can enjoy what is right and decent in continual prosperity." Our inherited gifts and legacies. Our true home, wherever it may be.

Ethel may be our physical home and/or our spiritual home. It can also mean an inheritance, an estate. When it lands face-down in a reading, it may indicate a change in our home, some difficulty at home, or one who is away from home. Sometimes it means a messy house when it lands face-down. *Key phrases:* home, inheritance, estate, roots.

Ac (oak tree): "The oak feeds the pig for meat for the sons of men. It often journeys over the gannet's bath. The ocean tests whether the oak keeps honorable faith." The oak is the tree of free will.

No one judges how the oak gives its gifts, except the ocean. Therefore, we may each choose how to give our gifts to the world and be our own witness. "Druid" translates as "being close to the oak tree." *Key phrases:* free will, self-direction, choice, taking responsibility, independence.

43

Aesc (ash tree): "The ash, precious to men, is very tall. Firm on its base, it keeps its place securely though many men attack it." The ash tree represents the Earth. The Earth keeps its place securely in the heavens although many people attack it. When each of us transforms our own consciousness, we transform Mother Earth; then it will truly be "on Earth as it is in Heaven."

The last letter of the *Futhorc* is the tree of death and transformation. *Aesc* means to return to the earth. The ash tree can also represent Yggdrasil, from which Odin hung to learn of the runes. Transformation indicates a spiritual change. In astrology, *Aesc* would be likened to the energy of Pluto. *Key phrases:* big changes, transformation, inner awakening, ego surrender, beingness.

The Wishing Stone: It is with our wishes that we design the future. Strangely enough, in the Anglo-Saxon *Futhorc* there was no rune for the Moon. Yet the Moon has always been an important symbol and archetype, especially in Goddess mythology. Our Moon, which faithfully orbits around the Earth, is the giant wishing stone of all time. Therefore, the Wishing Stone represents the Moon. The Wishing Stone is like a Carte Blanche of the universe (without interest charges). It amplifies any stone it falls near and never lands upside-down or face-down because it is blank.

CHAPTER V

MAKING YOUR OWN RUNESTONES
AND CLOTH

The runestones and rune circles you will need in order to perform a reading can be obtained commercially (my own *Rune Magic* sets are available from the address given in the back of this book). However, some people feel a closer kinship with the runes if they make their stones and circles themselves. In this chapter I will offer a number of methods which my friends and I have developed over the years for constructing your own stones and circles. Feel free to try whichever seem most suitable to your needs and resources.

MAKING THE STONES

There are a number of ways to create a set of runestones, and all are valued equally. The traditional method is to find a small branch of an oak tree and cut it into twenty-seven small, cylindrical pieces. Then the surfaces are smoothed with sandpaper and the runes etched on one side with a wood-burning tool or knife. Finish these by staining the runes with ink or paint.

Make it a practice to meditate on each rune as you mark it into your wooden "stones." Notice what ideas and images each suggests as you contemplate it. This will help deepen your understanding of the rune and place you more deeply in tune with your own stones. Your runes will be more valuable to you and will serve you better in your readings.

Another method for creating runestones is to visit your favorite beach and collect twenty-seven pebbles from along the shore. Select rocks not more than an inch in diameter and with relatively smooth sides. If you have access to a rock tumbler, you might tumble them for a while to make them smoother. Use a diamond scribe, easily obtainable from a lapidary shop, or a Dremel tool for electrically engraving the runes. After you have etched the runic characters into the stones, you may want to fill in the letters with white wax to make them more legible.

Yet another method involves drawing the runic symbols onto smooth, dried lima beans, using india ink and a very fine pen. You can also cast a set of runes in clay, but it must be well-fired so the pieces will not break easily.

Regardless of what you use for runestones, they must be small enough so that you can hold them all in your hands at once; they also must be heavy enough so that they won't bounce off the cloth when you cast them.

Some people even make runestones out of semiprecious stones, such as agate, quartz or jade. These turn out very beautifully, but I do not recommend this practice. For one thing, these stones are light in color and often semitranslucent, which makes it difficult to read runic letters carved or painted on them. For another, semiprecious stones possess special psychic properties all their own and these can throw off or obscure a reading.

My own first set of runestones was made using Apache

Tears, which are small, smooth pieces of obsidian. They are readily available at lapidary shops or can be picked up off the ground in New Mexico and Arizona. Apache Tears are named in memory of the tears shed by the wives and children of the Apache Indians, whose men were killed in battles with white men who came to fight with them for their lands. When one takes stones from Mother Earth, one should ask her permission, take them with gratitude and thank her.

The type of stone I use in the sets of runes I produce and sell are small Japanese beach pebbles. They are one-half inch to three-quarters of an inch in diameter and are pre-polished. They are available in gray as well as black and are found in garden stores or floral shops that carry Japanese Bonzai plants. They are generally too hard to inscribe with a diamond scribe, but an electrical engraving tool works pretty well if you use a diamond nib. You can also mark the runes onto these stones with a metallic pen, either silver or gold. If you use this method, coat the stones with several coats of liquid acrylic.

Do not try to coat the stones with varithane or any other polyurethane finishes, as they will dissolve the metallic markings. No matter which method you use, from time to time your stones will need refinishing. Each time you rescribe the stones, you make them more your own.

You may also want to keep your runestones in a natural-fiber pouch (velvet works well) or in a wooden box lined with felt or velvet. If possible use violet cloth, as this color serves to purify your stones between readings so that you don't carry one client's vibrations over into the next reading. In addition, you may want to keep a small amethyst quartz crystal or two in your rune box or pouch. This will also keep you runestones pure between readings, enhance the readings and deepen their meaning.

MAKING THE CLOTH

At one time the *Vitka*, or rune mistress, read the oracle by drawing a circle on the ground and casting her runes in the circle. The reading was determined by where the stones landed in the circle. Contemporary practitioners use a rune cloth. The rune cloth described in this chapter is taken from an ancient Celtic design (see Figure 2).

FIGURE 2
The Rune Cloth

You may want to make your own rune cloth, or perhaps you already have a special magic cloth which would work as a map of consciousness. I recommend a cloth with three sections, but if you have a better system, use it.

When I first began using the runes, I used a handkerchief, brightly colored in a Pakistani design, which was divided into three progressively smaller squares. The inner square (or circle) represented the Self, the middle square or circle represented the Ego, and the outer square represented wishes and potentials.

The inner circle, like your inner being, is basically clear. The only things which enter into your inner being are what you put there: God, your Spirit Guides (protection), love, meditation and any of the other symbols represented by the runes.

The second circle represents the ego or life in the outer world. At the outer edge of this circle there should ideally be one point of entry and exit—an opening in the maze. This can represent birth, death or transformation, although not necessarily in a literal sense. If a rune lands on this node, it is to be seen as a metaphor, a symbolic representation of that moment in time, and not a message foretelling a fixed event or destiny. Remember, you always have a choice in such matters.

According to this design, you could trace a maze of Light for twelve cycles before coming back to the starting point. Twelve is a symbolic number in the runes just as it is in astrology. Twelve is the number of houses in astrology, and one could also use the rune map to represent these houses. In the Tarot, twelve is the number of the "Hanged Man," one of the symbols of Odin, and Odin had a council of twelve.

You may also notice that each one of the sixty Celtic knots is different and unique. We each have a choice in life, as represented by the rune cloth, either to travel the path of Light, or to become entangled in the knots. Like the Celtic knots shown in the design, life is blessed with many paradoxes which defy logic. Paradoxes are God's way of playing "hide-and-seek" with us. When we can accept the

49

knots for what they are, rather than trying to figure them out, we are again free to travel the path of Light. Isn't en-*lighten*-ment simple?

The outer ring is composed of a continuous intertwined braid of three sections, symbolizing the power of the Law of Three in the universe. This law corresponds to the Druid concept of "trifold transformation," represented by the last rune (ᚠ), *Aesc*. Three also represents Hermes Trismegistus and the Holy Trinity in Christianity. The rune cloth has three sections, and 3 times 3 equals 9 (the number of nights Odin hung on the Yggdrasil), while 3 times 9 equals 27, the number of runestones.

The outer ring can also correspond to Jung's collective unconscious or the "collective conscious." The collective conscious can sometimes mean the "status quo" state of mind. But I see it as that realm of conscious knowing shared with our higher minds. Some may call this the "superconscious." The outer ring can also be seen as the Wishing Ring, because when we wish for something with the power of three, it manifests with greater certainty.

The rune cloth pictured in this book is a perfect mandala. A mandala is a sacred diagram, usually circular, often a circle within a square. Throughout history, mandalas have been used as meditation devices in many different cultures to both represent and promote psychic wholeness. The center of a mandala always represents the self, and because of their circular design, mandalas help to focus your attention on the center. Thus, mandalas are excellent devices for centering your attention inward through contemplation. Jung used mandalas in his own inner explorations and had many of his patients draw and paint them as part of their therapeutic process.

BLESSING THE RUNES

When I made my first set of runestones, I felt it important to bless them before I used them. The ways to bless your runestones are personal and varied. Intuition was my guide, and I exposed the runestones to the four basic elements. I immersed them in rich mud, allowed them to dry in the sun, washed them in pure water and dried them once again, this time in the air. I vowed to use them only for people's good, to illuminate the positive aspects of their lives.

Every year before the Renaissance Faire, I renew this ceremony of blessing—each time in a slightly different way. Last year, I washed and dried them and placed them outside overnight to be bathed in the light of the full moon.

Sanctify your runestones in your own way, as your inner being dictates—it is totally a personal matter. And remember, when you bless your runestones, they bless you in return.

CHAPTER VI

HOW TO READ THE RUNES

> *Whenever you stumble over the stones that lie in your path, remember that you're the one who put them there in the first place.*
> —Josephine Taylor

Hold all twenty-seven runestones in both hands. Close your fingers over the stones. Notice the weight and feel of the stones. Try to attune yourself to the many forces and concepts the runes represent. If there are any specific issues in your life on which you wish to focus, ask the runes to reveal what you need to know. But whether you have a specific question or just want a general reading, ask the Highest Source in the Universe to guide your casting and bless you with the wisdom to interpret it.

When you are ready, gently cast the runestones together onto the cloth. Remember that if you cast them from too high a level, they will bounce and scatter in all directions. If you drop them from too low a place, they will probably land in a heap.

It may take some experimentation to make all the stones fall right and stay on the cloth, but you'll soon get the knack of it. Above all, do whatever feels right to you and they will land in the most perfect way.

If you are reading the runes for another person, have them sit opposite you and pour the runes into their cupped hands. Next, have them focus on their question or concerns and ask the runes for guidance and wisdom. Then have them toss the stones onto the cloth. Follow the instructions given in this chapter to interpret the reading.

A more introverted type of person will tend to cast the runes toward the center of the cloth, which represents the self, and all the runes will land in one large cluster. The more extraverted personality will tend to cast the runes into the middle and outer rings, and fewer runes will land in the center. People who are reasonably balanced between introversion and extraversion will usually cast the runes evenly over the cloth, in the two innermost rings.

At first the runes on the cloth may look like nothing more than a random mixture of stones, but keep focusing on them. Even if your spread seems jumbled to you at first, you will soon begin to notice patterns. Read the runes according to their patterns, clusters, lines and constellations. Each rune is a separate thought. Notice which runes are connectors between one thought and another.

Which runes lie nearest the center? Which lie by themselves? Are there other constellations of rune patterns that suggest themselves to you (i.e., small squares or circles, etc.)? Some of these patterns may be continued from one circle to another. This simply means that there is an integration between elements or aspects of the self represented by these circles. This is normal and healthy.

I call straight lines of runes ''lines of power,'' and I believe that they indicate particular strengths of the person being read for. These strengths are composed of the elements represented by the runes making up the lines. Whenever the runes lie in straight or curved lines, read them together like a sentence or paragraph.

Sometimes runes may land in isolated sectors. Look for less obvious relationships and note how these runes relate both to you and to each other. Even if the pattern seems vague to you, if your intuition suggests a shape, don't block it out. You don't need to be psychic to read the runes, but you do need to use your intuition. Take your time and make your first rune-casting, (and for that matter, every rune-casting) a meditation.

The conscious and unconscious aspects of personality can be measured by the way the runes fall onto the cloth. Those stones which land face-up represent the conscious aspects of the subject's life or personality. Those stones which fall face-down tend to relate to the less conscious aspects of the subject's self. In turning the stones face-up as they are read, the subject becomes more aware of the less conscious, or latent, aspects of their personality at any given moment.

This is one of the most important ways in which the runes promote growth, transformation and healing: by leaving no stones unturned, you have the opportunity to bring to consciousness all the shadowed elements in your life. Looking at all the facts—positive as well as negative, conscious as well as unconscious—you can learn to accept, harmonize and harness them, becoming a saner, healthier individual in the process.

Often when the runes land face-down, they merely indicate information temporarily blocked or hidden from consciousness at the time—or simply aspects of a situation which require no conscious attention, perhaps because all is going well in that area, while other problem areas are clamoring for attention.

Next, consider into which of the three rings the individual runes have fallen. Each circle represents one of the triune aspects of the human personality: the inner circle, the Circle of Inner Being, represents the self of the person being read for; the middle circle, the Ring of Manifestation, or Ego

Realm, represents the manner in which the subject inter-faces with or manifests themselves in the world; and the outer circle, the Wishing Ring, represents their deepest hopes, wishes and desires. (See Figure 3.) When a rune lands within a circle, it indicates that the archetype or idea symbolized by that rune is operating in that area of the person's life.

First notice which runes have landed in the Circle of Inner Being. If there is one particular stone in the very center,

RUNE DIAGRAM

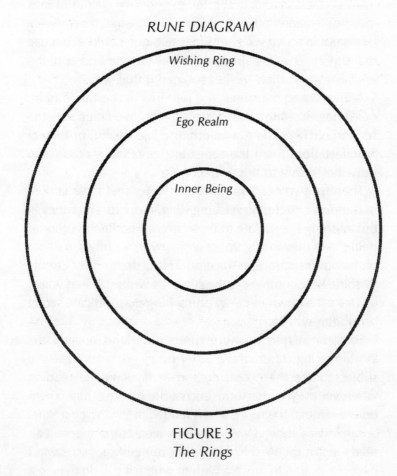

FIGURE 3
The Rings

it represents the hub of your wheel of life. If there are no runes in the very center of the cloth, or if most of the runes have landed in the Circle of Inner Being and seem to be in a jumble, begin with the rune or runes closest to the center.

The very center of the rune cloth is called the Center of Being. It represents the core or foundation elements of the subject's personality or character—the essence of their being. Runes which land there indicate the basic dynamics underlying the subject's life.

When the Circle of Inner Being is entirely clear, this may mean two different things: It could mean either that the subject is not in touch with her inner self, or it could also mean that the inner self is already clear of turmoil and conflicts and that the subject wishes to keep it that way.

After reading the runes and patterns in the Circle of Inner Being, examine the stones which have fallen into the second circle of the rune cloth, the Ego Realm, or Ring of Manifestation. Read the runes in this circle according to how they relate to the subject's ego.

Then turn your attention to the runes that have landed in the outer circle, or Wishing Ring. How do the runes in the Wishing Ring relate to those in the Ego Realm or Inner Being? Are they in alignment with any other runes in either of the other sections of the cloth? How do the runes in the Wishing Ring compare to the subject's wishes? Runes which landed face-down in the Wishing Ring may indicate secret or hidden wishes.

Sometimes one or more runes may land outside the Wishing Ring. After all the other runes are read, have the subject place these outside stones back in the reading wherever they wish. At the end of the reading, have them do the same to the runes which landed in the Wishing Ring. Sometimes a subject will wish to leave a stone where it already lies in the Wishing Ring. But remember, you always have the option to move a wish to where it will do the most good. People are often surprised by this option, and I always remind them that they're the ones who put their wishes where they are in the first place.

When a rune lands along the axis that passes from the center of the rune cloth straight up through the center of the top, it is said to lie on the "mid-heaven." In astrology, elements on the mid-heaven are said to represent a dominant influence in the subject's life.

In reading the runes for another person, you may tend to translate them symbolically. Keep in mind the context of the entire reading when trying to find the relationship of one rune to another. Sometimes the symbolic meaning is appropriate, but at other times a more literal translation is required. That is where you must trust your intuition. When I first began reading the runes at the Northern California Renaissance Faire, I did a reading for a gentleman who came to my booth. In this reading there was a cluster of three runes together in the upper left part of the Ego Realm: (M) *Eh*, work, (ᛟ) *Os*, communication, and (ᚦ) *Thorn*. I said, "Your work has to do with problems in communication, or the mouth. Are you a speech pathologist?" "No," the man replied, "I'm a dentist." This was a case in which the runic interpretation was quite literal in describing the man's profession. At other times the interpretations are more subtle and symbolic.

LISA

Reading the runes annually for people can be very revealing, a kind of chart of their yearly progress. A good example of this is shown in two readings I interpreted for Lisa, a friend who lives in another state and has sent me diagrams of her birthday castings two years in a row. Although there are significant changes between these two readings, there are also many similarities, indicating the constant or untransformed elements in her life.

The first reading (see Figure 4) shows a scattered quality to the runes, extraverted and with little focus, while the second (see Figure 5) shows greater organization and a more positive attitude. In the first reading many of the runes fell in the Wishing Ring or off the cloth altogether, indicating elements for which Lisa was still wishing, but which had not yet manifested themselves in her life.

In the very center is (ᚺ) *Haegl*, opportunity, and next to it (ᛚ) *Eoh*, the masculine energy. As Lisa is a Sagittarius, this in an appropriate place for (ᚺ) *Haegl*, for Sagittarians thrive on

RUNE DIAGRAM

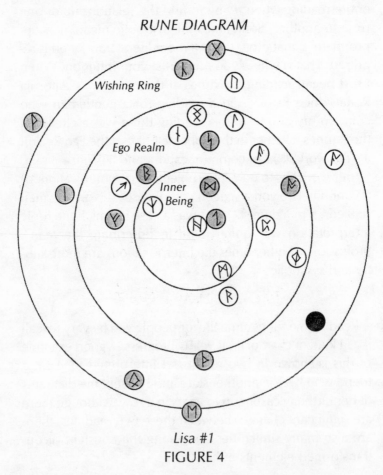

Lisa #1
FIGURE 4

opportunity. Notice that this rune lies in the center of both readings. Just next to (ᚻ) *Haegl* is (ᛇ) *Eoh*, the masculine energy, face-down. Also in the Circle of Inner Being are (ᛗ) *Mann*, people, (ᛞ) *Daeg*, meditation, and (ᛉ) *Eolh*, Spirit Guides. These show that opportunities are burgeoning but that her male energy is putting a damper on things, keeping her from moving out toward communication with others. The triangle formed by (ᚻ) *Haegl*, (ᛞ) *Daeg* and (ᛉ) *Eolh* shows a strong spiritual direction in her life, which Lisa needed to develop through the discipline of meditation.

RUNE DIAGRAM

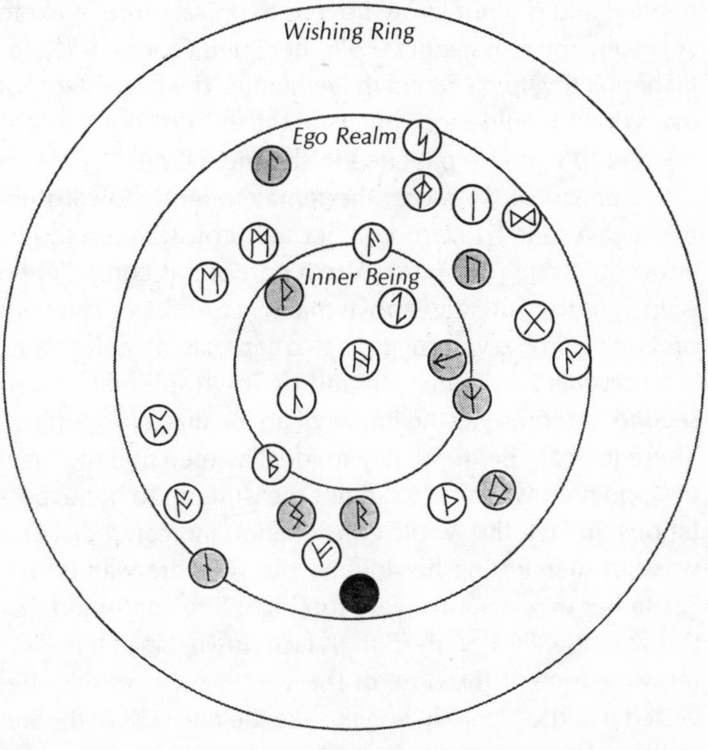

Lisa #2
FIGURE 5

Just outside the inner circle, in the Ring of Manifestation, or Ego Realm, is (ᛒ) *Beorc*, the feminine energy, also face-down. (ᛇ) *Eoh* and (ᛒ) *Beorc*, the male and the female, both face-down, represented Lisa's relationship with the man in her life, which was not working well at the time. They seemed to be going in two separate directions. Although there was still love between them, Lisa was feeling somewhat depressed about her inability to act decisively in the matter.

Also in the Ego Realm is (ᚠ) *Feoh*, face-down. Although Lisa was working at the time and held a responsible position in a company, she was not earning the income she needed and did not know how to manifest more. Next to (ᚠ) *Feoh*, and also near (ᛉ) *Eolh*, her Spirit Guides, is (ᛏ) *Tir*, faith, pointing to (ᛒ) *Beorc*, the feminine. This suggested that everything would work out all right for her, but that she needed to exercise patience in the meantime.

Just ahead of (ᛒ) *Beorc*, the female energy, toward her mid-heaven, is (ᚾ) *Nyd*, conflict and constraint, and just above it, (ᛝ) *Ing*, the hero. Also a part of this constellation is (ᛋ) *Sigil*, the Sun, and above that (ᛚ) *Lagu*, love. The hero on Lisa's mid-heaven suggests two separate meanings: first it represents her higher self and her own spiritual power; second, it represents the image of an idealized love object. These indicate her tendency to idealize men and then feel disappointed when they did not measure up to her expectations. In fact, the whole constellation indicated that Lisa was not manifesting her love in the way she wanted because her expectations were too high. She confirmed that this was true. (ᛋ) *Sigil*, the Sun, is face-down. Since this reading was done at the time of the winter solstice, this suggested that the blocks in her life, like the darkness of the sun at the solstice, were temporary.

However, nearby is (ᚫ) *Aesc*, transformation, upright and

unblocked. Further down in the Ego Realm is (ᛦ) *Peordh*, the child, which I thought represented her creative energy, but Lisa said it represented her son, who was about to be married. Since (ᚠ) *Ger*, abundance, marriage and commitment, are close by, I might have guessed this.

(ᚩ) *Os*, communication, is face-down, which I felt was somehow closely related to (ᚫ) *Aesc*, transformation. I told Lisa that as her spiritual self awakened, her problems with communication would begin to clear up. Just beyond (ᚩ) *Os*, in the Wishing Ring, is (ᚪ) *Ac*, free will. This suggested a wish for better communication with her son, her boyfriend, and as I later found out, with her ailing but very domineering mother, who was visiting her from Europe.

In the lower part of the Circle of Inner Being and partly into the Ego Realm are (ᛗ) *Mann*, the people, family, and (ᚱ) *Rad*, travel. At the time Lisa was looking forward to traveling to her son's wedding and seeing her family.

At the very bottom are three runes in her Wishing Ring, all face-down: (ᚦ) *Thorn*, the thorns, (ᛟ) *Ethel*, the home, and (ᛗ) *Eh*, work. These represented hidden difficulties entangling her at work and home. With a domineering mother and a boyfriend who tried to run her life both staying with her, this configuration seemed self-explanatory. (ᚪ) *Ac*, free will, was also in the Wishing Ring. I felt it could represent her longing for control of the situation. Also in the Wishing Ring, on the lower right side, is (◊) the Wishing Stone.

At the very top of the Wishing Ring are the runes (ᚳ) *Cen*, the path, (ᚷ) *Gyfu*, relationships, giving, and (ᚢ) *Ur*, the physical self. These runes suggested her desire to find her way on her path, which was blocked, and heal her relationships before the situation began to affect her health. (ᚷ) *Gyfu* actually lies off the cloth, and I felt that although it meant forgiveness, it was Lisa's way of trying to rid herself of those relationships which were not working out well. (ᚹ) *Wynn* (joy) has also fallen off the cloth. When you throw away relationships, you throw away the opportunity for joy.

It is interesting to note that all the runes in Lisa's Wishing Ring, including the ones she threw off the cloth, were face-down, with the exception of (ᚫ) *Ac*, free will. The advice I gave her was to have patience, stay with her situation and explore the other avenues open to her, as indicated by the strong community triangle with opportunity in its center. I told Lisa to focus on the positive elements in her life and let go of the negative; but like the dark sun, to remain low-key and not make hasty changes until she was more sure of herself. I told her it was time to plant the seeds of transformation by making conscious wishes for these things she wanted to harvest later in the year.

One year later, Lisa's rune reading (see Figure 5) shows far more definite lines and patterns, indicating greater clarity and more direction in her life. The Circle of Inner Being holds the same number of runes, but they are aligned in a more positive way. As in the previous year's reading, (ᚻ) *Haegl*, opportunity, occupies the Center of Being, showing that Lisa had not lost any of her Sagittarian opportunism. Just above it, to the right, is (ᛇ) *Eoh*, the masculine energy, face-up this time and not blocked. Just below (ᚻ) *Haegl*, to the left, is (ᚳ) *Cen*, the path, which leads downward to (ᛒ) *Beorc*, the feminine, just leaving the Circle of Inner Being and emerging into the Ring of Manifestation, or Ego Realm. (ᛒ) *Beorc*, the feminine, leads to (ᛝ) *Ing*, the hero, face-down, and beyond that, (ᚠ) *Feoh*, prosperity, face-up. Near them is (ᚱ) *Rad*, travel, change, next to (ᚠ) *Feoh*, prosperity, and beyond both of them lies (◊) the Wishing Stone. All these runes seemed to be saying that Lisa was taking her first tentative steps into the world, but was not yet really feeling her power, and that she will go through many changes and will prosper when she finally comes into this power.

Also in the Circle of Inner Being are (ᛏ) *Tir*, faith, and (ᛉ) *Eolh*, the Spirit Guides, who seem to be telling her to have faith in her center. Behind these two runes, but in the Circle of Manifestation, are (X) *Gyfu*, giving, relationship, and (ᚪ) *Ac*, free will. Not surprisingly, this year Lisa is free from the worst of the relationship problems she was experiencing last year and seems to be more in control of her life, as indicated by the balance shown between her masculine and feminine, which were in serious misalignment the previous year.

Just outside the inner circle, in the Ring of Manifestation, is (ᚫ) *Aesc*, transformation. It lies close to her mid-heaven and face-up, indicating a consciously directed effort to change. Nearby, face-down, is (ᚢ) *Ur*, health. Lisa was not having health problems, but she was selling health products, a difficult job. Above and to the right are four runes, all face-up, which seem to be related to (ᚫ) *Aesc*, transformation: (ᛋ) *Sigil*, the Sun, (ᛄ) *Ger*, abundance, (ᛁ) *Is*, vision, clarity, and (ᛞ) *Daeg*, meditation. This grouping seems to say that Lisa will gain clarity through meditation—a positive transformation, indeed. These four runes felt like a string of clear lights shining upon her.

Face-down, at the upper left of the Circle of Inner Being, is (ᚹ) *Wynn*, joy, and above it, in the Ego Realm, is (ᛗ) *Mann*, the people. Although her relationships with others were clearing up, they still had some ways to go. Above and also face-down is (ᛚ) *Lagu*, love, which like joy, remained somewhat hidden from her. Below (ᛗ) *Mann* is (ᛖ) *Eh*, work, and Lisa's current work was with people. I told her that she should strive to accept the love and joy her associations in work and play could bring her.

Continuing downward from (ᛖ) *Eh*, work, is (ᛈ) *Peordh*, creative energy, the child, and (ᚩ) *Os*, communication, followed by (ᚾ) *Nyd*, conflict, face-down, telling her not to worry about the difficulties in creatively communicating on her path out in the world.

At the bottom of the Ego Realm, near (ᚱ) *Rad*, travel, is (ᚦ) *Thorn*, the thorns, pointing to (ᛟ) *Ethel*, home. In our phone conversation following the reading, I asked Lisa what this might mean. Her mother, she told me, was not well and had gone back to Europe. Lisa felt frustrated that she could not afford to visit her, which may also explain why (ᚱ) *Rad*, travel, is face-down.

Lisa's second reading seemed a lot more positive than that of the previous year. She had taken many concrete steps in her life, partly as a result of the information she received from her previous reading. Lisa also seemed willing to take more chances in life and was benefiting by the risks she was taking.

In the second reading, there were virtually no runes in Lisa's Wishing Ring, indicating that she had achieved many of her goals from the previous year. The fact that (ᛏ) *Tir*, faith, (ᛉ) *Eolh*, her Spirit Guides, and (ᚹ) *Wynn*, joy, were all face-down in this reading does not suggest difficulties in these areas, but suggests instead that these forces were acting as hidden helpers. Lisa's relationship problems have also changed since the previous reading. Although she still maintains a friendship with her former lover, they no longer live together, and her masculine energy is freer, as is her feminine energy without her dominating and dependent mother in her home.

ALEGRA

Alegra was a thoughtful lady who came to me for a reading at the local Renaissance Faire. She was very poised and very real, and appeared to be in her late fifties. Although she cast all the runes, I have only drawn the most important ones here. (See Figure 6.)

RUNE DIAGRAM

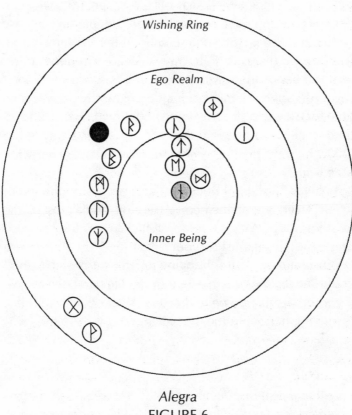

Alegra
FIGURE 6

In the very Center of Being lies (ᛏ) *Nyd*, conflict or constraint, face-down, next to (ᛞ) *Daeg*, meditation, (ᛗ) *Eh*, work, on its side, (ᛏ) *Tir*, faith, and (ᚲ) *Cen*, the torch. I took these five runes to mean that Alegra should not worry, but rather should meditate, focusing on her inner work and trying to have faith in where her path was leading. Just outside the Center is (ᚧ) *Ger*, abundance, and (ᛁ) *Is*, her viewpoint, indicating that there was much abundance in Alegra's life and that she could now manifest her vision in the world.

Near these, in the Ring of Manifestation, lies another constellation of runes, almost snake-like in shape: (Y) *Eolh*, guidance, (ᚢ) *Ur*, physical self, (ᛗ) *Mann*, people (in this case family), (ᛒ) *Beorc*, the female, and (◊) the Wishing Stone. Just beyond that is (ᚱ) *Rad*, travel. Alegra was about to retire, and her children were grown and had families of their own. Although she had been a doting mother, it was now time for Alegra to stop worrying about her children and attend to her own needs and desires. She was being led to follow her own deepest wishes to travel and fulfill her feminine self.

As I was finishing, I noticed two runes just to the left of where Alegra sat, on the hem of the cloth and almost off the Wishing Ring. Without noting which runes they were, I said, "Oh, those must be your signature." The runes were (X) *Gyfu* and (ᚹ) *Wynn*, bringing joy in relationships, and I could see that her gift throughout her life had been to give joy to others just by being herself. Alegra confirmed this, telling me her name means "giving joy."

KEITH

Keith is a healer, carpenter-painter and weaver who came to see me for a past-life regression. He has worked hard to develop himself spiritually and is deeply involved with his family. Since he had no specific question, I asked Keith to cast the runes to see where we needed to focus. (See Figure 7.)

The rune closest to the Center of Being is (ᚹ) *Wynn*, joy. Just below it, also in the Circle of Inner Being, is a cluster of three runes, face-down: (ᛋ) *Sigil*, the Sun, (ᚾ) *Nyd*, constraint, and (ᛗ) *Mann*, people, family. I felt this was a message that Keith need not worry as much about his family as he had in the recent past. Upward and to the right is (ᚢ) *Ur*, health, face-up, and Keith's health is good. Just beyond are

RUNE DIAGRAM

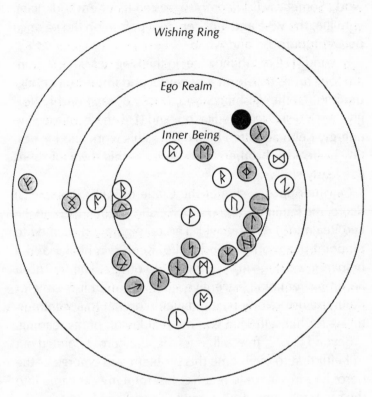

Keith
FIGURE 7

four more runes, all face-down: (|) *Is*, vision, (↑) *Lagu*, love, (ᚻ) *Haegl*, opportunity, and (Y) *Eolh*, the Spirit Guides. This seemed to suggest that the time was not right for him to form a love relationship and that he was keeping pretty much to himself. All this Keith confirmed. Just above (ᚢ) *Ur* is (ᚱ) *Rad*, travel, and next to it is (♦) *Ger*, abundance, face-down. Keith was planning to travel soon, but hadn't yet saved all the money he needed. At the top of the inner cir-cle is (ᛗ) *Eh*, work, face-down, and next to it lies (ᛦ) *Peordh*, the inner child, or the wise fool. Keith was between homes, unsettled like a vagabond, yet serene and productive in his work. Somehow (ᛈ) *Peordh* suggested that he was dancing with life, the wise and innocent fool poised on the balance between purpose and whim.

Beyond (ᛄ) *Ger*, abundance, in the Ring of Manifestation, are four runes that form a powerful and important configuration: (◇) the Wishing Stone, (X) *Gyfu*, relationship (forgiveness), (ᛞ) *Daeg*, meditation, and (ᛇ) *Eoh*, the masculine energy. Keith admitted he felt it was his work and his destiny to heal his brothers and sisters, as this string of runes so clearly shows.

On the opposite side of the Circle of Inner Being is (ᛒ) *Beorc*, the feminine, and (ᚦ) *Thorn*, and beyond these in the Ego Realm, (ᚪ) *Ac*, free will. This configuration seemed to pinpoint the problems in his life. Keith is a healer and a helper, good at giving out energy to others. The (ᚦ) *Thorn* lies in his feminine, receptive side. Although it is easy for Keith to nurture others, it is difficult for him to accept nurturing for himself. That was the real lesson of his reading.

Beyond (ᚪ) *Ac*, free will, is (ᛝ) *Ing*, the hero. I pointed out to Keith that to overcome this problem and emerge as the hero, he must learn to receive. Just then my cat came into the room for some strokes and I showed him how cats give just by receiving.

Close by in the Ego Realm is another cluster of runes, all face-down: (ᛟ) *Ethel*, home, (ᛏ) *Tir*, faith, and (ᚫ) *Aesc*, transformation. Keith was due to visit his parents in the near future, and I told him to have faith that things had changed for the better with them. This interpretation was reinforced by the fact that (ᚳ) *Cen*, the path, is near this constellation, and (ᚩ) *Os*, communication, lies right where Keith stood.

In the Wishing Ring is (ᚠ) *Feoh*, prosperity, seeming to lead out from (ᛝ) *Ing*, the hero. I felt this represented Keith's need to prosper by receiving for a change.

RICHARD

Richard, a financial counselor and single father, is quite spiritually evolved. His rune casting (see Figure 8) was as precise as the way he thinks, very methodical and intellectual. Another unusual aspect of this reading is that most of the stones are face-up, indicating how much of their message was devoted to consciousness in this person.

RUNE DIAGRAM

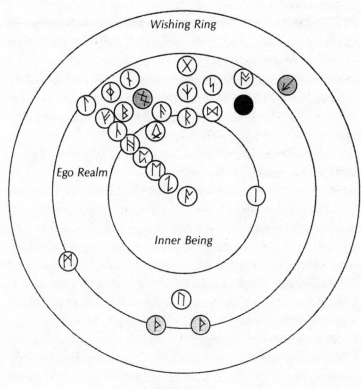

Richard
FIGURE 8

In the Center of Being is (ᛗ) *Ac*, the oak, the tree of free will. With someone as intellectual as Richard, I suspected the Center must represent his head, and that (ᛗ) *Ac* indicated he had reached a point where he could freely make whatever choices or changes in life he wished. Richard's son Edward, who was with him, confirmed this. Edward, then thirteen, was about to move back in with his mother, allowing Richard a freedom he hadn't had in years.

The fact that (ᛁ) *Is*, the eye (as well as I), is looking out into the world from the viewpoint of the inner self, reinforces the image of the center of the inner circle as his head. If we continue this analogy, at the bottom of the Ring of Manifestation three runes seem to represent Richard's ego or physical body: (ᚢ) *Ur*, the physical body, flanked by (ᚦ) *Thorn* on one side and (ᚹ) *Wynn*, joy, on the other. Spartan as it is, this is an appropriate image for Richard. Just on the cusp of the Circle of Inner Being, yet apart from the rest of his life, is (ᛗ) *Mann*, the people, reflecting the active role others play in his life and business.

Neatly stacked above the Center like blocks are strings of interconnected runic patterns and lines which seemed to represent Richard's current thoughts and concerns. Reading upward they are: (1) *Eoh*, the masculine energy, (ᛗ) *Eh*, work, (ᛈ) *Peordh*, child, (ᚻ) *Haegl*, opportunities (pleasure), (ᚲ) *Cen*, torch, (ᚠ) *Feoh*, prosperity, and (ᛚ) *Lagu*, love. Free will, the male energy, work, the child and opportunity all lie within the Circle of Inner Being, whereas the torch, prosperity and love all lie within the Ring of Manifestation. However, this configuration does not easily explain itself until we consider the others.

The rune (ᚻ) *Haegl*, opportunity, seems to mark the turning point from the inner self out into the world. The runes that follow it form a second line: (ᛟ) *Ethel*, the home, (ᚱ)

Rad, travel, (ᛞ) *Daeg*, meditation, and (◇) the Wishing Stone. Richard took this line to represent the change of direction in his own life brought about by his son's leaving. (ᚲ) *Cen*, the torch, represented the many new opportunities to move along his own path.

In the first perpendicular line (ᚹ) *Peordh* represented his son traveling to a new home and Richard's own prayers and wishes for his son. But (ᚹ) *Peordh* also represented the child in himself being allowed to come forth once more, now that he could relinquish the father role for awhile.

Next to (ᚲ) *Cen*, the light on the path, is (ᛒ) *Beorc*, the feminine, and next to that, face-down, is (ᛝ) *Ing*, the hero, while tucked in between (ᛉ) *Eolh*, the protector (Spirit Guides), and (ᛝ) *Ing*, is (ᚫ) *Aesc*, transformation. To me this suggested a change in a relationship with a woman, and an opportunity to have it become powerful and intense once the feminine (either in himself or his girlfriend) achieved more of its power. Beyond (ᛉ) *Eolh*, the Spirit Guides, is (ᚺ) *Sigil*, the Sun, (X) *Gyfu*, relationships, and (ᛗ) *Os*, communication. This seemed to represent an abundance of friendship and communication in this relationship. These were counterbalanced by (ᛚ) *Lagu*, love, and (ᛃ) *Ger*, abundance, but also (ᚾ) *Nyd*, conflict, or more likely paradox. These runes suggested that the relationship held an opportunity for real closeness and intimacy, if Richard could accept the imperfections of his own anima, or "inner woman." If he could not, then the runes indicated that he would become entangled in conflict over differences between himself and his female partner.

Out on the cusp of Richard's Wishing Ring, face-down, is (↑) *Tir*, faith, pointing to his thoughts and indicating that he should trust his own intuition. Richard's reading also showed that he would have plenty of opportunities for an abundant and loving relationship once he could accept his own feminine energy and work out the conflicts in any unfinished relationships. That most of the runes were face-up indicates that Richard was extremely conscious of the process at work in his life and has a better than average chance of resolving any problems he might face. I recommended that he try bodywork in order to learn to live more fully in his body and less exclusively in his head.

CHAPTER VII

THE RUNES AND
SELF-TRANSFORMATION

*The borders of our minds are ever
shifting and many minds can flow
into one another . . . And create or
reveal a single mind, a single energy.*
—W. B. Yeats

TRANSFORMATION

The process of transformation is happening all the time, on all levels of the universe. Webster's *Unabridged Dictionary* defines transformation as the "act or operation of changing the form or external appearance; a change in condition, nature or function." This definition is totally accurate in relation to the outer world, but seems incomplete in relation to our inner self. Transformation involves not being merely the passive object of change, but also the conscious experiencing of that change when it takes place. For example, when we transform our inner attitude from poverty to prosperity, we begin to experience and manifest prosperity in our lives. (ᚠ) *Feoh*, prosperity, is the first of the runic symbols.

Scientists also recognize that change comes in three categories: structural changes, seasonal changes and changes in the order or magnitude of consciousness. For instance, transcontinental superhighways represented a structural change in the way traffic flowed across the U.S. But they also brought regions of the country closer and changed the way people perceived themselves and each other. This represented a change in consciousness. Sometimes one or more forms of change are precipitated by a prior change of a different kind.

Thus the process of transformation may be an evolving pattern made up of small increments of change over a long period of time, or it may be attributed to one single event. The events may be totally different, but the effect on our consciousness is the same. At first apperance, then, it can seem as if all transformation is instantaneous. But many long-term subtle changes may be an integral part of a transformation process, even when we are not able to recognize them. The same is true of rune readings. A single reading may change our life, or a number of readings may represent increments in the overall process of transformation.

Transformation can also occur when we redefine or reconceptualize the meanings of certain words and phrases. For instance, the runes (K) Peordh, the fool, or the child, and (X) Ing, the hero, may seem like two diametrically opposed archetypes. The hero, as an archetype, is often thought of as the powerful, successful achiever, and the fool as the silly clown or child. So how can the hero and the fool be one and the same? The answer would seem to be paradoxical but is actually very simple. The hero often represents the achiever who acts without love and/or wisdom, as Odin did when he became too greedy for power. On the other hand, the fool can often represent the wise creative child who stops to listen.

When (X) Ing, the hero (which also means "being in present time"), listens to the inner child for wisdom, then the hero and the fool become one in the deepest significance of the self. When the hero, the fool and the self are all in alignment, they become the foundation for higher consciousness, and at this level, miracles happen. If we substitute the masculine and the feminine for the hero and the fool, the same thing holds true.

TRIFOLD TRANSFORMATION

The catalyst causing change may be many different things, some of which may seem inconsequential at the time, but the change happens on three levels at once. Trifold transformation takes place when the catalyst that causes the change unifies all three levels of our lives at the same time.

Danaan Parry tells of an instantaneous transformation that took place when he was in Moscow a couple of years ago for a conference. Feeling somewhat like a "stranger in a strange land," he was hurrying through the Moscow train station one night, carrying two heavy and obviously American suitcases through the crowded, noisy, snowy passageway between trains. Suddenly Danaan looked up and saw a young Soviet engineer calmly cleaning the falling snow off a windshield. When the young engineer, with grease on his face, saw Danaan look up at him, he stopped what he had been doing and made complete and total eye contact with him. As Danaan described the incident, "It felt like this young man and I looked directly into each other for what seemed like eternity, transcending all barriers of cultural differences." Finally the engineer shouted down to Danaan over the noise of the diesel engines, in Russian, "I know you . . . you're just like me!" At that moment, time stood still for both of them and there was God seeing/knowing God! This is Trifold Transformation—a look and a mutual knowing coming from willingness and intention, at the deepest level, to communicate. Danaan and the Soviet engineer were both forever changed by that experience—and in some way, so were the United States and the Soviet Union.

In literature, an example of this concept can be found in Dante's trilogy, *The Divine Comedy*, a transformative journey of a soul through Hell, Purgatory and on to Paradise. Tolkien's classic tale, *The Hobbit*, is another example, which is even more closely patterned on the old Nordic/Druidic/Celtic myths about the runes. Didn't the dwarves find their way to the dragon using the runes on the map? Like Dante's *Divine Comedy*, the Tolkien work represents the transformation of an ordinary being (the hobbit) during a journey through the darkness of his own fears to become a hero to the world, and ultimately, to himself. In order for Bilbo and his friends to face the dragon, they have to confront their deepest fears and muster up all of their courage.

Within the concept of trifold transformation, it is obvious that the number three holds some special significance. Three is a symbol of wholeness: a triangle is the least number of lines that can enclose a space and one of the most inherently stable structures. We are all familiar with the Trinity in Christianity—the Father, the Son and the Holy Spirit—who represent three different stages in the transformation of a single energy. In Druid mythology, God was the Creator, the Sustainer and the Destroyer. In Goddess-oriented cultures, there is the "Triple Goddess": Hebe (the virgin), Hera (the mother) and Hecate (the crone). In Indian philosophy these are Kali's Triple aspects: *Parvati* (the virgin), *Durge* (the sustainer) and *Uma* (the crone). In Norse mythology there are the three Norns. Yggdrasil, the ash tree of transformation, had three roots which formed the foundation upon which the rest of Yggdrasil and its denizens flourished.

It is important to realize that in all these trinities one part represents the dark, or shadow, aspect of things. Self-transformation takes place when we are able to shine light on this shadow aspect, making ourselves conscious of it. By making the unconscious aspects in our lives conscious, a rune reading can become a catalyst in the overall process of transformation. Just as the rune cloth is a map of consciousness, the rune reading lays out all the elements on our path. By unifying these elements we can deepen our understanding of our own transformative journey through time.

Because the runes are set in a spiritual context, they help us to realize that we are first of all spirits who have minds to use and bodies in which to live. When we operate our lives from the viewpoint of spirit, we open doors for the Source, or God, to come through. Then God cooperates with us in miraculous ways to help us discover who we are and how we can best serve ourselves, humanity and Mother Earth.

ALICE

The following reading is an example of transformation resulting from a woman's conscious realization of the presence of an internal archetype which was in conflict with her perception of her mate. Alice is an intellectually sophisticated professional woman, who at the time of this reading was going through a temporary crisis in her relationship with her boyfriend (see Figure 9).

Only a few runes have landed in the Circle of Inner Being, and the stones closest to the center are face-down. There are also curves and strings of runes, indicating much consciousness and clarity in her life. The two runes closest to the center are (◊) *Ger*, abundance, and (ᛇ) *Eoh*, the masculine energy. This highly trained woman has an abundance of masculine energy which she incorporates very well in her work as a therapist, as well as in managing her life. *Eh*, (ᛗ) work, between her Inner Being and her Ego Realm, validates this.

RUNE DIAGRAM

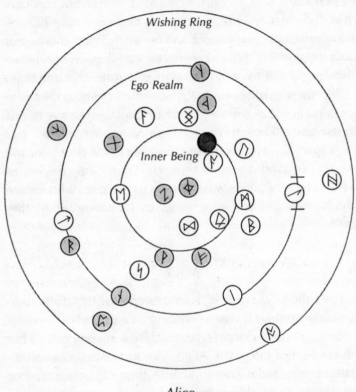

Alice
FIGURE 9

The runes which lie face-down in this reading are the ones which outlined her problem to me: (X) *Gyfu*, face-down in the Circle of Manifestation, or Ego Realm, indicates that her love relationship was not working well at the time; also in the Ego Realm, just below the Circle of Inner Being, are (Þ) *Wynn*, joy, and (Y) *Feoh*, prosperity, both face-down. This indicated that her ego was not in tune with her inner being at the time and was preventing her from having a more fulfilling life.

On her mid-heaven is the rune (ᛝ) *Ing*, the hero, face-up, but next to it is (ᚦ) *Thorn*, the thorns, face-down; above that, also face-down, is (ᚲ) *Cen*, the path. This constellation shows that although Alice was the hero in her own world and capable of acting, internal thorns were blocking her path and she felt lost. Also in the Ego Realm is (ᛒ) *Beorc*, the feminine energy, next to (ᛗ) *Mann*, the people. This reflected her desire to live in a more extroverted manner than her relationship with her mate allowed.

Alice's insight came when she realized that her conflict on one level was that she did not want a man in her life because she was basically in love with her own animus, her internal masculine side, and felt at that time that her mate could not compete with this side of herself. This phenomenon has been called the "Annie Oakley Syndrome."

In another part of the Ego Realm, just at the entrance/exit point on the rune cloth, is (ᛚ) *Lagu*, love, and just beyond that, in the Wishing Ring, is (ᚻ) *Haegl*, opportunity. This sequence reflected both her desire to let go of the relationship and her desire to correct the situation harmoniously. From the lower left side, (ᛏ) *Tir*, faith, points to her work and her inner being, telling her to have faith in her inner process.

At the upper left side, in the Ego Realm, just above the Inner Being and face-up, is (ᚫ) *Aesc*, transformation (a very positive sign), between (ᚷ) *Gyfu*, face-down, which could mean forgiveness, and (ᛝ) *Ing*, face-up, the hero. (◊) the Wishing Stone is next to (ᚪ) *Ac*, free will, indicating that she was in control of her own path.

Once Alice realized how much she loved her own inner masculine side, she was able to let go of it and transfer that love to the masculine side of her mate. Her insight helped transform her relationship without giving it up. She discovered that it was all very well to love her own inner archetype, but it couldn't keep her warm on cold nights.

CHAPTER VIII

RUNES AND RELATIONSHIPS

THE ELEVEN PRECEPTS OF RELATIONSHIPS

Relationships are the building blocks of a sane and mature society. Each of us is in a relationship with our self, with God and with one another, whether or not we wish to acknowledge or honor that relationship. Our evolution as a people depends upon our conscious awareness of how we conduct relationships and the recognition of our basic interdependence upon God and one another for love, support, communication, commerce and family.

Often when we think of relationships, we think of *romantic love*. Relationships can all be loving, though most are not romantic: for instance, the relationship between business associates, parent and child, teacher and student, or therapist and client. But even within the context of romantic love, what do we mean by love and how can we express it in the most beneficial way?

Relationships can often lead us into a tangle from which we despair of finding a way out. However, if we keep in mind the following "Eleven Precepts of Relationships," we can avoid or mitigate many of these problems.

These precepts came to me one morning many years ago during a meditation. I had been asking for some laws of relationship, since at that time I had been unable to sustain a relationship with a mate. I did not originate all of these statements; most of them I had heard from various teachers at one seminar or another. But that particular morning they all came tumbling into my mind like Moses receiving the Ten Commandments. Over the years I have shared them with many, as I now share them with you.

THE ELEVEN PRECEPTS OF RELATIONSHIPS

1. The nature of all relationships is paradoxical.

2. Our first and most important relationship is with our self.

3. We are all mirrors. What we want from another is our self. What we can give to another is their self.

4. The purpose of relationships is to position our self in the world.

5. Relationships are vehicles for sharing experiences and for expressing feelings.

6. The key to intimate relationships is honest communication.

7. Relationships need space, harmony and rhythm in order to grow.

8. Relationships cannot grow without individual expansion and growth.

9. The quality of relating is far more important than the form a relationship takes.

81

10. We can't really have a relationship unless we are willing *not* to have a relationship.

11. Relationships never end, only their forms change.

Most of these precepts are self-explanatory. *The nature of all relationships is paradoxical* came to me once as a huge revelation. I used to wonder why my relationships seemed to go along smoothly for awhile, and then suddenly my partner would seem like a perfect stranger to me, and perhaps I to him. Each of us have variables in our personality that we reveal from time to time; but sometimes we see the other person's "shadow side," or they see ours. When we make the commitment to love another person, we also make a commitment to accept their shadow side, and it behooves us to be mindful of this aspect before entering into a relationship. If both parties know from the start that such paradoxes are implicit in relationships, they will not be shocked or confused when one rears its unfamiliar face.

Actually, paradoxes are great teachers. They get our attention by their captivating twists. They are a way of making sense out of confusion and seeming conflict. The secret beauty of paradoxes is that when we accept them for what they are, they act as a tool for getting in touch with our higher self. Paradoxes make form and structure out of the grist of conflicts and for that reason alone are to be respected. They are not limited to interpersonal relationships, but are an integral part of all relationships in the universe. Without paradoxes, the world would be static and not dynamic. Think about it!

The second precept states that *Our first and most important relationship is with our self.* If we do not honor that relationship, listen to our inner wisdom, nurture ourself and take care of our most basic needs, we will not have the ability to relate intimately to someone else.

Recently, while trying to complete this manuscript, I had an experience which allowed me to achieve a deeper sense of my relationship with myself. I had been going through a painful period of financial difficulty and had been feeling really down and out. I could not access my creative energy for writing and I was not even earning enough money to pay my rent. I was worried about taking care of my most basic needs and even more worried about meeting my deadline on this book. Needless to say, I was quite depressed.

One night I woke up at 4:30 A.M. and knew that I ought to meditate, but I had to get up at 6:00 A.M., so I decided to sleep a bit longer instead. Just as I closed my eyes, a voice began to "talk to" me mentally, and I recognized the voice as my Spirit Guide, Monal. He said, *"You don't have to sit up and meditate, because I'm going to talk to you lying down. Now hear me! It's as if there are two Deons. Your lower self Deon, and your higher self Deon. We need your higher self to work with, and your lower self is getting in the way by being unsettled and depressed. Your lower self has got to go now or we can't work with you, and we really need you. If you want to find the job you want, if you want to finish your book, if you want your relationships to work and even if you want a car that runs, you had better shape up!"*

I thought about my car. It had been a gift from a special friend and had served me well for more than four years. Now it was falling apart and no longer felt safe, but I didn't have the money to fix it properly. The previous morning my daughter Amara had told me about a dream she'd had in which she was driving my car over the Golden Gate Bridge and had a blowout. She said that in the dream, it had been the right rear tire that blew; and when she looked at it, she saw that it had a big hole down to the threads. I neglected to check my tire that morning.

That evening I had to run a short errand and Amara came

with me. While driving, I had an eerie feeling that I could have an accident and drove very carefully. When we arrived home, we heard a hissing sound which we discovered was my right rear tire going flat. As we changed the tire, we discovered a hole completely through the rubber down to the threads! The hole was on the inner side of the tire, where it had gone unnoticed.

Then Monal said, *"Remember Amara telling you about her dream yesterday? That was no dream. We were trying to forewarn you and we couldn't get through to you, so we told Amara."* I thought again about the whole incident with my car, how I had sensed that I might have an accident, how I hadn't checked my tire after Amara's dream and how I had probably been driving on that bad tire for weeks without even realizing it. I could easily have had a blowout on the freeway. Having the flat right in front of my house was fortunate, and I realized how merciful my guides had been with me. It may have been just coincidental, but I believe our guides really do play an active part in helping us in our lives.

That morning when I woke up, I was transformed. I gave up caffeine (once again). I got on with the business of finding work, and very soon after, a miracle happened. I received a phone call from a friend who knew of a company that needed help with a special project. When I stepped into this office, I knew it was exactly what I had been looking for and my financial troubles were abated.

I had the time and space to complete my manuscript and felt appreciated for what I contributed to that project. All this came out of correcting my relationship with myself, with God and with my Spirit Guide.

There is a sequel to this story. On the way to the office that first Saturday morning, the water pump in my car broke. There were no mechanics I knew of who were open on Saturday, so my car sat on the street all day. Then on Sunday, someone in the office knew of a mechanic who came Monday morning and fixed my car right on the street. When the mechanic was finished, he told me about an inexpensive car in excellent mechanical shape and several years newer than my car. With my old car as a trade-in, the new car cost me very little, and I now have a safe, well-running sports car.

During the years in which I've been sharing my "Eleven Precepts," the statement that people puzzle over the most is the one which says: *We can't really have a relationship unless we are willing not to have a relationship.* This concept illustrates the lesson of attachment/non-attachment which the yogis and Zen Masters teach. Sometimes young couples fall in love and feel that they cannot live without each other. Then when they mature further as individuals, they may grow more independent of each other, sometimes to the point where they choose to go their separate ways and actually break up.

However, there is a space in relationships in which both people realize their own self-sufficiency. They do not feel an unhealthy "need" for their partner. Instead, each knows how to be alone and happy, yet realizing that life is more enjoyable when shared with the other.

The runes can be used with individuals, couples and organizations to show quickly and without judgment any potential problems or areas of conflict, allowing those involved to reframe them into a more positive context. When left to our own devices, we tend to blow incidents and illusions way out of proportion. The runes provide a method of seeing more clearly into the many paradoxes in personal and business relationships and the uncomfortable situations in life where we tend to get stuck. The runes can make molehills out of the mountains of misunderstandings we

create, and with their wisdom, can unravel the entangle-
ments of thorny relationships. By shining the runic light of
consciousness onto the variables and miscommunications,
we can refocus awareness on the positive aspects of a relationship while letting go of the illusion of the negative.

Just as you can read the runes for an individual, you can
read the runes for a couple or those involved in any relationship—lovers, friends, parents and children, even business partners.

To do a relationship reading, those involved (if possible)
should sit side by side, close enough for each of their outer
hands to be cupped together. Place the runestones into
their cupped hands and have them formulate the question
together or ask for a blessing. When they are ready, have
them cast the runestones, in concert, onto the cloth.

Those runes which fall in the innermost circle represent
the inner being of the relationship. The middle ring, of
course, represents the physical plane of the relationship,
while the outer ring represents mutual goals or wishes.
Sometimes a rune will land closer to one person than the
other; it will probably pertain to that person, offering clues
to their position in the relationship. Those runes which land
face-down represent aspects of the relationship hidden from
the participants before the reading began. Any runes that
land outside the Wishing Ring can be randomly tossed back
onto the cloth, or consciously placed wherever the couple
chooses.

As with most other readings, begin with the rune closest
to the center. This, more than any other, will define the
strongest factor in bringing or keeping the couple together.
Interpret these runes as you would any other rune reading,
keeping in mind that it pertains to a journey together,
whether for a day, a year, a lifetime or many lifetimes.

Following are several sample relationship readings. The

first illustrates the second of my precepts: *Our first and most important relationship is with our self.* Although this reading seemingly only involves one party, it actually involves two. The person being read for (in this case, me) and my higher self.

DEON

It is not often that I read the runes for myself. I am almost too familiar with them and what they have to say. However, while going through my most recent period of discouragement, financial strain and writer's block, I did cast the runes (see Figure 10).

This reading seemed to suggest good organization (many of the runes lined up across the Circle of Inner Being) and clear consciousness (many of the runes landed face-up). On the other hand, the runes in the Center of Being were all face-down, indicating my current area of unconsciousness. In the very center is (ᛈ) *Peordh*, the creative child. Next to it, face-up is (ᛗ) *Ac*, free will, followed by and continuing to the left, (ᛏ) *Tir*, faith, (ᚦ) *Thorn*, the thorns, and (ᛒ) *Beorc*, the feminine. Above *Beorc* is (ᛋ) *Sigil*, the Sun, and below (ᛒ) *Beorc* is (ᚲ) *Cen*, the light on the path.

In this reading the creative child in the Center of Being was somehow blocked. The feminine receptive force was also somewhat suppressed. The "mother" part of myself was not nurturing the inner child. Yet surrounding the feminine, (ᛋ) *Sigil*, the Sun, is (ᚲ) *Cen*, illuminating my path. This suggested that it was important for me not to lose faith because of the obstacles in my path. It looked as if the universe was all set to help me, and all I had to do was correct my relationships so that I would be ready when things began to happen. Just beyond the feminine, in the Ego Realm, is (ᚷ) *Ger*, abundance, and (ᛇ) *Eoh*, the masculine energy.

RUNE DIAGRAM

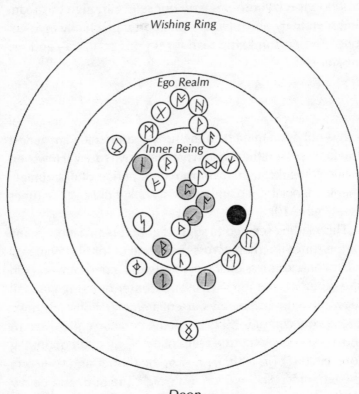

Deon
FIGURE 10

This confirmed what my Circle of Inner Being seemed to be saying: that just beyond my center lay abundance, if only I would acknowledge my inner feminine-receptive self and focus my masculine-assertive self out in the world.

On the other side of the creative child, (⟨) *Peordh*, also face-down, is (↑) *Lagu*, love, and (⋈) *Daeg*, meditation. *Daeg* is face-up, suggesting I try consciously meditating, and from there the path forked out in two directions. On one hand is (Y) *Eolh*, the Spirit Guides, and on the other is (F) *Aesc*, transformation, leading to (P) *Wynn*, joy, (N) *Haegl*, opportunity, (ᛟ) *Os*, communication, and (X) *Gyfu*, my gifts to (ᛗ) *Mann*, the people. The runes indicated that I did not need to worry about my home, because deep in my inner being there would be a change, (ᚱ) *Rad*, in my prosperity, (ᚠ) *Feoh*.

From the above sequence, I could easily see how my Spirit Guides were working with me to remind me that my inner child needed not only love, but also discipline (through diet and meditation), which was necessary to bring about the needed change in my affairs. Through meditation my path would be transformed, bringing joy and the opportunity to share my gifts with other people.

Just before me, in the Circle of Potentials, is (ᛝ) *Ing*, the hero, my persona, and just above (ᛝ) *Ing*, is (ᛁ) *Is*, my vision or viewpoint, face-down. This seemed to reflect my feeling of not knowing exactly where I was going. Next to (ᛁ) *Is*, are (ᛗ) *Eh*, work, and (ᚢ) *Ur*, health. Near (ᚢ) *Ur*, just inside the Circle of Inner Being, is (◊) the Wishing Stone. This seemed to represent my wish to put my best self forward in the world, to manifest my vision in a positive way through the kind of work I wanted to do, and to complete my manuscript—all in good health and good time.

This reading was very positive and illuminating and helped me see clearly where my inner self had been. In spite of the chaos I was experiencing, I saw a lot of order in my life. I saw that by making all these aspects of my inner self conscious and keeping the faith, everything would manifest itself in good time. Three days later I found work.

SUSAN

The next reading demonstrates the truth of my precept, *We can't really have a relationship unless we are willing not to have a relationship.*

Susan is a minister and healer who uses her bookkeeping and managerial skills to help run a cooperative store in the Bay Area. On the occasion of this reading, Susan was celebrating her fortieth birthday, which was her coming-out party. For the past six years Susan had maintained a fairly low profile, keeping within a small circle of friends. Although many people have loved her, Susan kept herself free of intimate, romantic relationships during this time, while consciously working on her relationship with herself. Her reading suggested that she was definitely ready for a breakthrough.

First of all it is interesting to note that the shape of Susan's reading (see Figure 11) looks very much like a sunburst, with a cluster of runes in the center and many spokes generating outward like the rays of the sun. In the very Center of Being is the rune *Ing* (ᛝ), the hero (which she truly is), and next to it are (ᛗ) *Eh*, work, and (ᚩ) *Os*, communication. In her life and work she has always been a communicator. Then, just below those three runes, are (ᛒ) *Beorc*, the feminine, and (ᚠ) *Ac*, free will, with (ᛋ) *Sigil*, the Sun, right in the middle. Then (ᛉ) *Eolh*, the Spirit Guides, and next to that (ᛗ) *Mann*, the people.

Radiating out from (ᛒ) *Beorc*, her feminine self, into the Ego Realm are two runes, both face-down. These felt to me as if they represented a question she was asking. The first is (ᛏ) *Nyd*, conflict, which when face-down means there is no need to worry. The second is (◊) the Wishing Stone. I told Susan she was not to worry about her femininity anymore, as she truly is a radiant woman.

Also in the Ego Realm, just below (ᛉ) *Eolh*, representing her Spirit Guides and face-up, are (ᚢ) *Ur*, health, (ᚱ) *Rad*, travel, and beyond those, in the Wishing Ring, (ᛇ) *Eoh*, the masculine energy. I told her that her Spirit Guides were blessing her with good health, and that she would be traveling somewhere to meet the man for whom she had been

RUNE DIAGRAM

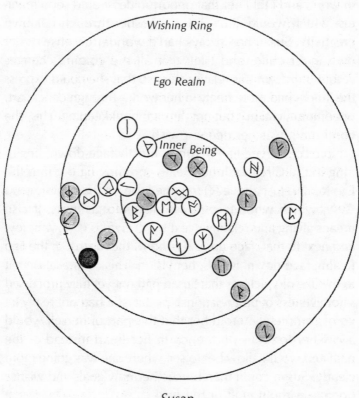

Susan

FIGURE 11

wishing and preparing. This sequence, combined with the sequence radiating out from (ᛒ) *Beorc*, the feminine, seemed to indicate what her forty-first year was about. Note that (ᚩ) *Os*, communication, precedes (ᛇ) *Eolh*, the Spirit Guides, indicating that she had been communicating with them, and that they were with her, blessing her on her birthday.

A cluster of four runes on the right, in the Ego Realm, all seemed to be related. They were (ᚨ) *Aesc*, transformation, (ᛟ) *Peordh*, the child, (ᚺ) *Haegl*, opportunity, and (ᚠ) *Feoh*, prosperity. At the time, Susan was looking for a new kind of work, and I told her that opportunities would soon manifest which would allow her to prosper through her own creativity. Susan has always had a wonderful sense of her own inner child, and I felt that all the coming changes would transform this relationship, so that she could express the inner child more freely in her work—through dance, art, or communication—but not through bookkeeping. This, she confirmed, was her deepest wish.

Note the curved line of runes, mostly face-down, beginning in the Circle of Inner Being and moving out into the Ego Realm. Just above (ᛝ) *Ing*, the hero, in the center, is (ᚷ) *Gyfu*, which when face-down means forgiveness. It also means giving and relating. Next to (ᚷ) *Gyfu* is (ᚹ) *Wynn*, joy, and next to that, face-up, is (ᚦ) *Thorn*, the thorns. In the Ego Realm, face-down, is (ᛁ) *Is*, her vision. This constellation felt to me like old pictures that Susan had not yet fully processed —forgiveness of past relationships that she had not really let go of completely. I told her that this part of herself would allow her to focus on the joy in her heart instead of the pain and would allow her to see where she was going more clearly. Susan could then pursue her new goals and wishes openly, without guilt or remorse.

Another spoke radiated out of the Circle of Inner Being near the point of her ascendent: just above (ᛒ) *Beorc*, the feminine, and wedged between that and (ᛗ) *Eh*, work, is (ᚲ) *Cen*, the light on the path leading to (ᛚ) *Lagu*, love; beyond, sitting within the Ego Realm, is (ᛟ) *Ethel*, the home, while down from (ᛟ) *Ethel* is (ᛞ) *Daeg*, meditation, which culminated in (ᛜ) *Ger*, abundance and commitment. This suggested that the path from her own center would lead to an abundant, spiritual, loving home, whether it was her present home or a future one. Then, appropriately enough, right on the point of the cloth at which the serpent bites his tail—

the one opening in the labyrinth of life—is the rune (↑) *Tir*, faith. Susan had learned her lessons well.

This reading gave a clear, positive picture of where Susan had been and where she was headed at the time of her fortieth birthday. It is a good example of how *You can't really have a relationship unless you are willing not to have a relationship.* Susan had spent the last six years not having a relationship, practicing self-reliance, healing herself of negative emotions and low self-esteem, so that now she was ready to open the floodgates of life with a trusting and loving heart.

MICHAEL AND ANN

The following reading is probably closer to a typical relationship reading than the first two examples, since it includes a couple in a love relationship.

A few months ago, Michael and Ann, a very talented young couple, came to me for a reading. They are both fine artists and craftspeople. They had been sweethearts as well as business partners for a number of years. Lately, however, their relationship had become rocky. He thought he wanted a different woman and she thought she wanted a different man; but in talking with her, he discovered that she actually didn't want a different lover, she just needed to be wanted as a lover.

I had them sit next to each other and poured the runestones into their combined hands. They closed their hands and quietly asked their inner questions, then allowed the runestones to scatter onto the cloth (see Figure 12). Some of the positions in this first reading are indicated by [1].

The runes landed with a straight line (line of power) coursing through the Center of Being, in alignment with where Ann was sitting. (1) *Eoh*, the masculine energy, is in the very

RUNE DIAGRAM

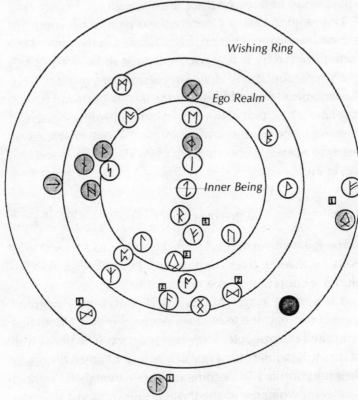

Michael and Ann
FIGURE 12

center, face-up, indicating that the strength of this couple was currently in their business relationship. Just below (ᛇ) *Eoh* is (ᚱ) *Rad*, travel, as there is a lot of travel involved in their work. Just above (ᛇ) *Eoh* is (ᛁ) *Is*, the vision or viewpoint, and just above that, face-down, is (ᛄ) *Ger*, abundance. Above (ᛄ) *Ger* is (ᛗ) *Eh*, work, and above that (in the Ego Realm and face-down) is (ᚷ) *Gyfu*, giving and relating.

(ᛁ) *Is*, the viewpoint, is blocked and (ᛄ) *Ger*, abundance, is hidden from them. (ᛄ) *Ger* also stands for commitment in relationship, and perhaps this too was blocked; all they could see was their work.

In another section of the Inner Being is (ᛚ) *Lagu*, love or the emotions, and beyond that, (ᛈ) *Peordh*, the child. Both of them have children they love who are not at this time living with them, and (ᛦ) *Eolh*, the Spirit Guides, seem to be watching over them. Also in the Inner Being is (ᚢ) *Ur*, health, face-up, and they are both in good health.

(ᛋ) *Sigil*, the Sun, is shining on their Inner Being, yet integrally related to a constellation in the Ego Realm, made up of the runes (ᚦ) *Thorn*, (ᚾ) *Nyd* and (ᚻ) *Haegl*, all face-down, which appear to be clouds on the horizon made up of thorns and conflicts. (ᚾ) *Nyd* face-down means there is nothing really serious to worry about, so I told them not to focus on their problems but to try to see them as creative opportunities. By consciously looking at their problems, they could transform them.

Just beyond and pointing toward that particular constellation is (ᛏ) *Tir*, faith. Just above that is (ᛗ) *Os*, communication, face-up and not blocked, and beyond that, near the Wishing Ring, is (ᛗ) *Mann*, the people, which might represent counsel, family or friends. This configuration indicated that their ability to communicate their problems to each other and outsiders was still unimpaired, as demonstrated by the fact that they shared their problems openly together and with a counselor (in this case, me).

Also in the Ego Realm and near where Michael was sitting is (ᛒ) *Beorc*, the feminine aspect; in this case, Michael, the one who is home the most, is the dreamer, a quality sometimes associated with the feminine. Also in the Ego Realm and close to Michael was (ᚹ) *Wynn*, joy, and (ᚳ) *Cen*, the light on the path. These runes suggested that there were no real obstacles on their path, only opportunities to embrace the joy in their lives. However, just in front of

Michael, in the Wishing Ring, lie (◊) *Ethel*, the home, and
(Y) *Feoh*, prosperity. Michael, who likes to stay home and
be creative, had prosperity in his own hands.

In front of Ann, in the Ego Realm, is (X) *Ing*, the hero, and
further toward the Circle of Inner Being is (ľ) *Ac*, free will.
Just in front of Ann, beyond the Wishing Ring, is (ľ) *Aesc*,
transformation. Ann's opportunity to act out the hero involved her occupation, traveling and showing their work.
In the Wishing Ring, right side up and close to Ann, is (⋈)
Daeg, meditation. This landed just beyond (Y) *Eolh*, the
Spirit Guides. I felt this configuration indicated the importance of meditating both with their Spirit Guides and with
their children. Since it is also in line with (ľ) *Lagu*, love, I
felt it was important to meditate about their love life as well
and suggested they read some books on Tantric love techniques. Also in the Wishing Ring, right between Ann and
Michael, is (◊) the Wishing Stone, indicating that their combined wish as a partnership was yet to be fulfilled.

I then suggested they move the runes which had fallen
closest to them, as well as those which had fallen out in the
Wishing Ring and beyond. (In Figure 11 and in Figures 12
and 13 which follow, I have indicated the original positions
of the runes by [1] and the places they were moved to by
[2].) They moved (ľ) *Aesc*, transformation, to be near (X)
Ing, the hero, and (⋈) *Daeg*, meditation. This made a
powerful triad. Michael then placed (◊) *Ethel*, the home,
near (ľ) *Lagu*, love, and (Y) *Feoh*, prosperity, next to (ľ) *Rad*,
travel, so that prosperity could come from their travels.

Then they confessed that they both hoped to buy a home
as soon as more money came in. At the moment they were
living in their studio, which was quite cramped and not very
romantic. Since they lived in the country, I told them to
meditate on a warm, cozy cabin near their studio, and it

turned out they had already found such a place, but did not yet have enough money saved to buy it.

I then did individual readings for both Ann and Michael, with both present.

ANN

Most of the runes fell into the Circle of Inner Being, a few fell into the Ego Realm and fewer still into the Wishing Ring (see Figure 13). Two runes lie face-down in the Center of Being: (ᚹ) *Wynn*, joy, and (ᚾ) *Nyd*, worry. Ann has the potential for joy, which shows in her inner being, but at the time she was too worried to experience it. Next to (ᚾ) *Nyd* is (ᚫ) *Aesc*, transformation, (ᚷ) *Gyfu*, giving and/or relationship, and (ᚦ) *Thorn*, all suggesting that Ann had been worrying about the need to transform her relationship with Michael. Also close to (ᚾ) *Nyd* is (ᛝ) *Ing*, the hero, and (ᚢ) *Ur*, health, indicating that Ann was strong enough to overcome her difficulties. In a part of this same cluster are the runes (ᛖ) *Eh*, work, and (ᛚ) *Lagu*, emotions, face-down, suggesting that she was so busy with her work that her emotions were suppressed. It was as if she felt she did not have the time to be in love with Michael or even to express her feelings, whatever they might be.

Just beyond this cluster, near (ᚦ) *Thorn*, the thorns, on the edge of the Ego Realm, are the runes (ᚻ) *Haegl*, opportunity, and (ᛏ) *Tir*, faith, indicating once again that opportunities were waiting just beyond her worries and that she must have faith in what lies ahead.

As in the first reading, (ᛈ) *Peordh*, the child, is near (ᛉ) *Eolh*, the Spirit Guides, and (◊) The Wishing Stone. I felt her guides were watching over her children, as her wishes indicated, including the child in herself. Between (ᛈ) *Peordh*

RUNE DIAGRAM

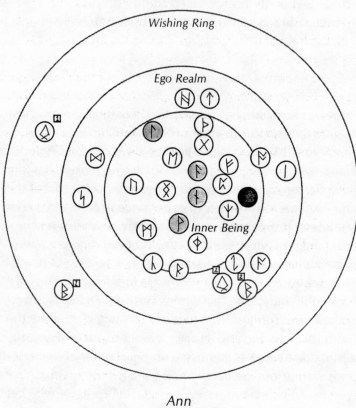

Ann

FIGURE 13

and (X) *Gyfu*, giving, is (Y) *Feoh*, prosperity. Near these runes, in the Ego Realm, are (M) *Os*, communication, and (I) *Is*, vision. These two runes so near to her Wishing Stone indicate a decision to bring her own creative vision out into the world, which Ann confirmed.

A constellation of four runes are also in the Circle of Inner Being, just below (P) *Wynn*, joy. Clockwise, these are: (♦) *Ger*, abundance, (R) *Rad*, travel, (K) *Cen*, knowledge, and

(ᛗ) *Mann*, people. These suggested that if she drew properly on her own inner resources and continued to travel in the service of their business, her work would reach the people.

In the Ring of Manifestation, or Ego Realm, on the lower right side, are (ᛇ) *Eoh*, the masculine energy, and (ᚨ) *Ac*, free will, indicating that Ann had control over her own masculine energy and the way it expressed itself in the world.

Face-up, on the left side in the Ego Realm, are (ᛋ) *Sigil*, the Sun, and (ᛞ) *Daeg*, meditation. If this were an astrological chart, these two runes would be on her ascendent. I felt this indicated it was important for her to spend time in meditation to ensure a positive attitude.

In the Wishing Ring at the upper left is (ᛟ) *Ethel*, the home. As in the previous reading, she was wishing for a new home. At the lower left of the Wishing Ring is (ᛒ) *Beorc*, the feminine energy, suggesting Ann's desire to balance this energy and find fulfillment. I suggested she move these runes (these wishes) any where she wanted. She moved both of them (positions [2]) directly below (ᛇ) *Eoh*, the masculine energy, and (ᚨ) *Ac*, free will, so that she could feel the balance between her masculine and feminine energies and use this to manifest the home they both wanted. This completed her rune reading. Because Michael was allowed to watch the reading and hear the interpretation, it clarified aspects of their relationship which he had not previously understood; most of all, to see Ann's thought process as spelled out with the runes.

MICHAEL

In Michael's reading, many of the runes landed upside down in the Circle of Inner Being (see Figure 14). But in spite of the fact that Michael seemed to be somewhat inner-directed, a fair number of runes also landed in his Ego

RUNE DIAGRAM

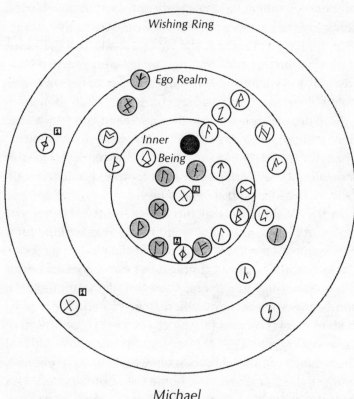

Michael
FIGURE 14

Realm. As with Ann, a couple of runes landed in the Wishing Ring and in almost the same location.

In the Circle of Inner Being, face-down, in almost the same spot as Ann's runes, is (ᛏ) *Nyd*, conflict. The other two runes, which also landed face-down to complete a triangle, are (ᚢ) *Ur*, the physical self, and (ᛗ) *Mann*, the people, which actually landed closest to the Center of Being. Even though Michael likes to keep to himself most of the time, people are his prime motivators. His craft, jewelry-making, is a very people-oriented trade. Near (ᛗ) *Mann*, the people, are the two runes (ᚹ) *Wynn*, joy, and (ᛗ) *Eh*, work, both face-down, indicating that he was not consciously experiencing joy in his work. But near (ᛗ) *Eh*, work, is (ᚠ) *Feoh*, prosperity, also hidden. At this point, Ann and Michael said they were working hard, but not reaping the harvest of their labor; they were experiencing a slump, both financially and emotionally.

However, next to (ᚠ) *Feoh*, prosperity, are (ᛚ) *Lagu*, love, (ᛒ) *Beorc*, the feminine, and (ᛞ) *Daeg*, meditation, all face-up. I told him that meditating on loving feelings with the feminine in his life would help increase his prosperity and creativity. In the Ego Realm, just beyond (ᛚ) *Lagu*, love, are (ᛁ) *Is*, vision, face-down, and (ᛢ) *Peordh*, the creative child. This indicated that meditating on his creativity would help him to see more clearly where he was going, so the child inside wouldn't feel so uncertain about the future. (ᚲ) *Cen*, the light on the path, is close by, and (ᛋ) *Sigil*, the benevolent Sun, shines where he hoped his path would lead him.

Next to (ᚾ) *Nyd*, conflict, is (◊) the Wishing Stone, and near that, (ᚫ) *Aesc*, transformation. On the other side of (ᚾ) *Nyd* is (ᛏ) *Tir*, faith. Michael's wish was to transform his inner conflicts, and the message was to have faith in his own abilities. In the Ego Realm, just beyond (ᚫ) *Aesc*, is (ᛖ) *Eoh*, the masculine energy, and just beyond that, (ᚱ) *Rad*, travel, the first of three runes very prominently placed in the Ego Realm. The second is (ᚻ) *Haegl*, opportunity, and the third, (ᛣ) *Ac*, free will. In fact, a fair was about to begin, giving both Michael and Ann the opportunity to travel and sell their wares.

At the left side of (ᚢ) *Ur*, the physical self, in the Circle of Inner Being, is (ᛟ) *Ethel*, the home, and nearby at the ascendent is (ᚦ) *Thorn*, indicating problems with their present home. However, out in the Ego Realm, near (ᚦ) *Thorn* and upright, is (ᚩ) *Os*, communication. Above (ᚩ) *Os* is (ᛝ) *Ing*, the hero, and just above (ᛝ) *Ing* is (ᛉ) *Eolh*, the Spirit Guides.

At first Michael did not understand (⊗) *Ing*. I explained that the hero represented his willingness to be his best, in his relationships with himself, Ann and the outside world. The fact that he was willing to talk with Ann about the problems in their relationship, without attempting to blame her for them, seemed to be a sign that he was willing to be the hero, and it looked as if his guides were also there to help him.

We then looked at (♦) *Ger*, abundance, and (X) *Gyfu*, relationship and giving, both in the Wishing Ring. Michael certainly had wishes for his relationships and for abundance. He moved (♦) *Ger* into his Inner Being, between (Υ) *Feoh*, prosperity, and (M) *Eh*, work—an appropriate place for abundance. To make positive his relationship between his worries, his health and demands of other people, he moved (X) *Gyfu* to the Center of Being, between (Π) *Ur*, health, (ᛗ) *Mann*, the people, and (♦) *Nyd*, worry. By turning all these runes face-up, he made a positive picture of something he could do to transform the way he utilized his masculine energy in the world, as was his wish.

When people are ready to hear, you don't need to say much in order to be understood. In checking with Michael and Ann two months later, I found their relationship had greatly improved. They had not yet moved into a new home, but their business was doing much better and they were happier together than they had been for a long time.

PUBLISHING ON DEMAND

In addition to focusing on personal relationships, the runes can be used for business relationships. The following reading (see Figure 15) involved the principals in a small publishing company called Publishing on Demand that was new and just getting off the ground.

RUNE DIAGRAM

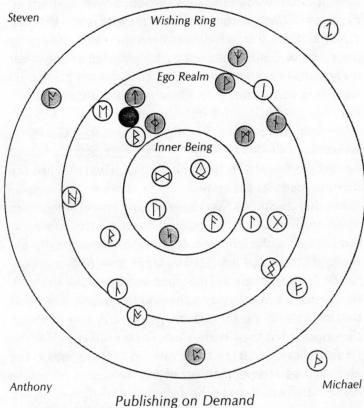

Publishing on Demand
FIGURE 15

Anthony, Steven and Michael, the three founders, held the runestones together and cast them onto the cloth. Many of the runestones landed face-up, indicating a high degree of consciousness and conscientiousness in forming the company.

Looking at the Circle of Inner Being, the inner workings of the company, we see first its physicality. The company is not just an illusion, a dream or a wish. It is real, it actually exists. To support its reality is (ᚢ) *Ur*, the physical. Also in the Circle of Inner Being is (◊) *Ethel*, the home—or in this case, the actual office in San Francisco. Between these two runes is (⋈) *Daeg*, meditation. Because (⋈) *Daeg* is between (⋂) *Ur* and (◊) *Ethel*, it indicates the importance of keeping the place of business sacred by keeping the energy clear and clean. The other rune in the Circle of Inner Being is (ᚠ) *Aesc*, transformation, indicating that what already exists is not static, but is in a dynamic process of growth. The fifth rune in the Inner Being is (ᛉ) *Sigil*, the Sun. The fact that it has landed face-down means that the parties involved could not yet see the effects of manifestation. The time, like the funding, had not yet come.

Another cluster of five runes lie just inside the Ring of Manifestation, or Ego Realm, close to where Steven was sitting: (ᛒ) *Beorc*, the feminine, (◊) the Wishing Stone, (ᛗ) *Eh*, the work, face-up; and (↑) *Tir*, faith, and (ᛜ) *Ger*, abundance, both face-down. This group suggested that the feminine process was currently active and that a birth was about to take place. It was through the feminine, creative, receptive aspect that their wishes would be fulfilled. Here the runes indicated that the three needed to have faith in the abundance to come, that part of their present work was to hang in there and await the coming birth.

Beyond this cluster, in the Wishing Ring, is (ᚠ) *Ac*, the oak tree of free will, suggesting that Steven was wishing his free will could exercise a greater part in making things happen faster. Coming down on the left side is (ᚻ) *Haegl*, opportunities to travel, indicated by (ᚱ) *Rad*; then farther down, (ᚲ) *Cen*, the light on the path, falling near (ᚠ) *Os*, communication, which fell slightly into the Wishing Ring. This indicated that they were hoping their business would foster greater communication, which is what publishing is about. If one follows this path of runes to the bottom, face-down in the Wishing Ring is (ᚹ) *Peordh*, the fool or the child (in this case, the company—the newborn in question).

Steve and Anthony are the actual founders. Michael is the manager. In the Ego Realm, close to where Michael was sitting, is (ᛝ) *Ing*, the hero, and just beyond that, in the Wishing Ring, is (ᚠ) *Feoh*, prosperity. Michael's efforts as manager place him in a position to play the role of the hero and pull the company together. Off the rune cloth, in front of Michael, is (ᚦ) *Thorn*, the thorns. This was appropriate, since Michael often acts as troubleshooter for the organization. The thorns, somewhat separate from the rest of the runes, may be a good sign, since it can represent creative opportunities.

On the right side of the cloth are the runes (ᛚ) *Lagu*, love, and (ᚷ) *Gyfu*, giving. This configuration reflects the real purpose of the organization: to serve the business community by offering the finest in high-tech electronics to support the publishing and printing business and the public at large.

Farther up on the right, face-down, are (ᛗ) *Mann*, the people, and (ᚾ) *Nyd*, conflict. They seem to say, "Don't worry, the people are on their way and will arrive when everything is set up." (ᛁ) *Is*, vision, is half-way in the Ego Realm and half-way in the Wishing Ring. This suggests it was important for them to stay focused on their vision. Just beyond those runes, face-down and hidden, are (ᚹ) *Wynn*, joy, and above that in the Wishing Ring, (ᛉ) *Eolh*, the Spirit Guides, who seem to be saying, "It's all happening. Be joyous!"

Paradoxically, the rune (ᛇ) *Eoh*, the masculine energy, like the thorn, lies off the cloth. This may seem curious since the principals of this company are male, but remember, the birthing process is largely a feminine one. However, if the masculine energy seems held in abeyance, this is an illusion. The three are all busily creating the home, the structure of the organization and the workflow, so that when the baby is actually born it will have a haven in which to grow.

CHAPTER IX

THE RUNES AND REINCARNATION

PAST-LIFE THERAPY

Many people also use the runes as an aid in recalling their incarnations in former lives and in healing or resolving problems in their current life that seem to stem from these past lives. Although this idea may seem far out, many highly respected psychiatrists, psychologists and academics in the mental health field have embraced it, and a number of them have formed the Association for Past-Life Research and Therapy.

However, one does not have to believe in reincarnation to benefit from PLT (Past-Life Therapy). Whether the past lives people remember are actual events or merely powerful metaphors that the mind has created, recalling these lives seems to have a profound healing effect on the subject's present-day psychological difficulties.

Due to their antiquity and the natural materials of which they are constructed, the runes are an almost ideal vehicle for tuning in on past lives. Often when I pour the stones into the hands of a client who has never seen them, the client experiences a sense of having known them "before." The runes can help a person gain access to past-life material in order to release long-repressed emotions, and to bring to consciousness deeply buried, obsolete decisions still affecting the person today. Besides deprogramming such negative karma, working with this material is also useful for getting in touch with hidden talents and skills which may lie dormant in a person's psyche.

Clients have remembered past lives in monasteries where they had learned art and calligraphy, and after the session went on to "relearn" these skills almost effortlessly. One client recalled being a famous musician, and following the session sat down at the piano for the first time in twenty years and extemporaneously played beautiful music which he composed on the spot.

Often a client comes to me wanting to find out who their "soulmate" was in a previous life, and/or whether or not they had a soulmate. Sometimes a rune reading will reveal things about the way a couple relates to each other in this life that give a clue to the karma they carry over from previous lifetimes together.

TOM AND GAYLE

Very recently, a young woman named Gayle, for whom I have read the runes every year for the last five years at the Renaissance Faire, came to me for a past-life reading for herself and her new boyfriend. Over the years, Gayle has transformed and grown from being an unhappy and confused individual into a highly evolved, loving, spiritual person whom many people love in return. Tom is a warm, personable, very bright and talented man, and he and Gayle seemed to be very well matched for each other. First I had them hold the runes together, then cast them on the circle. Tom sat on the left side and Gayle on the right, and the runes landed in a fairly symmetrical pattern (see Figure 16).

RUNE DIAGRAM

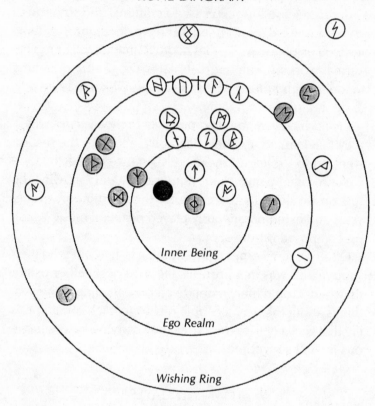

Gayle and Tom
FIGURE 16

In the Center of Being is (◊) *Ger*, abundance, commitment, face-down. This indicated that they have, at the core of their relationship, a rich, full sense of each other. (◊) *Ger* also means marriage and when face-down can give a hint of something that previously went wrong. Both Tom and Gayle have been married and divorced before, and were naturally cautious about committing themselves to their current relationship, although neither of them was conscious of this fact before the reading.

Also in the Circle of Inner Being, all face-up, are (ᛗ) *Os*, communication, (◊) the Wishing Stone, and (↑) *Tir*, faith, pointing to a group of runes in the Ego Realm which I felt had much to do with both their present-life relationship and those of past lives as well.

Since they had just recently begun living together, I could understand (ᚾ) *Nyd*, conflict, next to (◊) *Ethel*, the home, as there were certainly adjustments to be made. On the other hand, (ᛚ) *Eoh*, the masculine, and (ᛒ) *Beorc*, the feminine, as well as (ᛗ) *Mann*, the people or family, all form a harmonious cluster. What seemed curious to me are the four runes above these, one of them right on the entrance/exit point of the rune cloth. They are (from left to right): (ᚻ) *Haegl*, opportunity, (ᚢ) *Ur*, the physical self (on the opening), (ᚨ) *Aesc*, transformation, and (ᚲ) *Cen*, the torch, the light on the path. The fact that (ᚢ) *Ur* fell where it did made me curious to know how their past-life material might relate to the reading. (ᛝ) *Ing*, the hero, is on their midheaven in the Wishing Ring, representing a shared wish to emerge victorious from any current difficulties in their relationship.

Face-down in the Ring of Manifestation, or Ego Realm, is (ᛚ) *Lagu*, love, reflecting a focus on other aspects of their relationship that day. (ᛗ) *Eh*, work, and (ᛈ) *Peordh*, the child, are both face-down where Gayle was sitting. She had just moved, was looking for new work and was perhaps hoping for children if the relationship with Tom worked out.

On the right side of the Wishing Ring is (ᚹ) *Wynn*, joy, as well as (|) *Is*, viewpoint or vision. Since the latter lies right on the cusp between the Ego Realm and the Wishing Ring, this suggested a mutual clarity in the face of the unknowns of the relationship. Finally, (ᛋ) *Sigil*, the Sun, shines upon them from off the cloth.

On the left, where Tom was sitting, near the Circle of Inner Being, are four runes face-down: (ᛦ) *Eolh*, the Spirit

Guides, next to (ᛝ) *Daeg*, meditation, (ᚷ) *Gyfu*, relationships, forgiveness, and (ᚦ) *Thorn*, the thorns. To Tom, this
suggested that through meditation with his guides he could
clarify and forgive any past knots in his relationships, including the present one.

I then asked each of them in turn to meditate on the runes
and to talk about any past-life material they might bring up.
Tom was the first to speak. He recalled a very early lifetime
which seemed to pre-date Atlantis. He remembered living
in caves as part of an Amerindian tribe that led an extremely
simple life, close to the earth. During this early time, body-
forms were just making the transition from androgynous to
bisexual beings. Procreation was more by will, mating in
spirit, rather than body. Theirs was a matriarchal culture in
which knowledge was passed down telepathically from
mother to daughter. However, Tom, who was male in that
lifetime, had a close telepathic connection with his mother,
Gayle, and she broke the tribal precedent by teaching him
all she knew.

During that lifetime, Tom had lived very close to water
beings, such as whales and dolphins, who did not look
quite the same as they do today. These sea beings came
from other planets and had ways of communicating with
them. Humans were emanations of the Earth. From his
trance-like state, Tom said, "The ascent of the humanoid
forms is in direct proportion to the descent of the water
forms." The more the human population increased, the
more the sea-mammal population decreased.

Next Tom recalled a life as a senator in Rome in the years
just before the crucifixion of Jesus. He said, "Christ was a
political/spiritual revolutionary, threatening Rome and elimi-
nated by Roman law." He could see the changes taking
place as Rome destroyed itself through decadence. He himself was constantly tempted by the pull of pleasure.

In that lifetime, Tom knew Gayle as a beautiful young temple dancer consecrated to the goddess Diana. He was very much in love with her and persuaded her to break her vows of chastity to the goddess and marry him instead. They sailed away to Greece together in a galley. Once there, Gayle bore him a child, but the child died. Then she had another child, who also died. Tom then became a Christian, which upset Gayle, who still worshipped the goddess. In that lifetime, Gayle died very young, and Tom suffered many hardships. Eventually he retired to the hills of Italy, where he died of pneumonia.

Tom recalled another lifetime in Spain during the Middle Ages, when he was imprisoned as a religious heretic. Gayle had been his sister and had been burned at the stake as a witch. Their mother was Moorish and very knowledgeable in mathematics, architecture and early Egyptian teachings. Their father had been an alchemist and their parents worked together very closely, but aside from sharing their knowledge with their children, kept very quiet about what they knew. The children, Tom and Gayle, tried to teach this knowledge publicly and were imprisoned and put to death.

Just before he returned to his present life, Tom recalled another lifetime in Rome in which he was a Christian slave and Gayle a Roman who sent him to his death.

Tom spent some time forgiving all his past adversaries, and especially Gayle, who had left him in a number of past lives and had even caused his death in one. Tom said that he could now understand why they were together. He realized that part of the purpose of his present lifetime was to heal his relationship with Gayle. Tom felt he understood why at different times she felt like his sister or his mother or his teacher. She had been all of those during their past lives together.

Next, Gayle began to recall her past lives. Her first

memory was of an androgynous life among the Incas around 500 A.D. Gayle was not a member of the tribe, but a student of higher knowledge from another planet who had arrived in a spaceship. She came to Earth as a messenger to study love and intimacy and to take back this knowledge to those on her home world, a planet far larger than Earth. During her stay she met Tom and they fell deeply in love, but the time came all too soon when she had to return home and leave him behind.

Next, Gayle recalled a life as a German soldier during World War I. She and Tom had both been boys, best friends who grew up in a little village. Neither of them wanted to fight in the war, but it was expected of them. Tom was shot and died in Gayle's arms. She grieved very heavily, and although when she grew older she became a leader in her village, Gayle never got over the loss.

Then Gayle recalled a life in which she was a beautiful Arab dancer and lived in a harem. Tom, a wealthy Sultan, was her master and husband and her good friend. Although the Sultan had many wives, Gayle recalled that he grieved severely when she died.

Last, Gayle recalled a past life in Scotland during the 1700s during which she was a Celtic healer, midwife and herbalist. In this lifetime Tom was one of her children.

The lifetimes recalled by Tom and Gayle may have been real or metaphorical. But it is interesting to note that neither remembered any lifetime that the other remembered, yet there were many similar themes in both accounts. Tom and Gayle recalled countless lifetimes in which they had been deeply connected to each other, and as a result seemed to feel that at least part of their purpose in this lifetime was to complete their family experience together.

When we look again at their combined rune reading in the light of the past-life experiences each recalled, the four runes at the top of the Ego Realm seem to make more sense and seem to say that Tom and Gayle can transform their path in life together by conscious choice. Both Tom and Gayle recalled lives in which they were either from another planet, or were one of the early humanoids, just learning to live in a dense human body. They also recalled a number of lives in which either they died young, or their mate did. All of this gave them the feeling that the body is a very tenuous, temporary experience.

CHAPTER X

OTHER RUNE GAMES

In addition to casting the runes randomly upon the cloth, we can also lay them out in various patterns that can be used to represent specific situations (in much the same way that Tarot layouts do). In this chapter I will present six patterns, each of which is designed to facilitate or clarify certain kinds of readings. These patterns are: 1) The Pentagram, or "Wish Upon a Star," good for a general reading; 2) The Star of David, or "As Above, So Below," good for asking a specific question and receiving a specific answer; 3) the Cross, or "Groundpoint," excellent for helping find your center; 4) Infinity, or the "Path of Paradox," good when you are at an impasse in resolving a conflict; 5) The Interlocked Triangles, or "Meditation," helpful when you want to meditate on a specific problem and arrive at an expedient solution; and 6) The Triangle, or "Trifold Transformation," both the simplest and most abstract of all the diagrams, since the three corners are to be self-labeled according to your own circumstances, needs or wishes.

Also included is a "Game of Communication," which can be played with your family or a group of friends. It can be both fun and a revealing means of inner and interpersonal growth.

WISH UPON A STAR

The Pentagram (see Figure 17) is a good pattern to use when someone wants a general reading but does not have a specific question or issue in mind. The Pentagram must always be laid out with the peak at the top and the two points at the bottom.

For this layout choose eleven stones at random from the pouch and place one in the center position to represent the

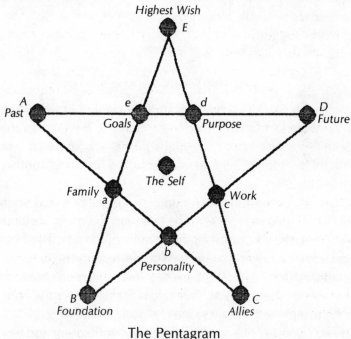

The Pentagram
or
Wish Upon a Star
FIGURE 17

Self or viewpoint. Then place the remaining stones face-down, in any order you choose, around the inner or Ego Circle and then around the outer circle, which represents the world.

Begin with the rune in the center. Note any parallels between its symbolism and your current self. Then turn over and read the runes in the inner or Ego Circle in the following order: (a) goals; (b) family; (c) personality; (d) work; and (e) purpose. Next turn over and read the runes in the outer circle in the following sequence: (A) the past; (B) the foundation; (C) allies; (D) the future; and (E) your highest wish. Finally, look over the whole reading for noticeable patterns, sharp contrasts or significant relationships. Also be sure to consider the whole for any overall impression or messages it might suggest.

AS ABOVE, SO BELOW

Use this Star of David diagram (see Figure 18) when you have a question to ask of your spiritual self. It is easy for the Source to answer our questions if only we know how to ask them. Remember that each solution becomes another question.

Choose seven runes at random and place one face up in the center (A) to represent the Self, and the other six face-down on the six corresponding points of the star. Then begin with the lower triangle, which represents the world of manifestation (E, F, G). Turn the lowest rune (G), which represents the physical, face-up. Next turn over the rune which represents knowledge (F), and then love (E).

The harmony of knowledge and love is wisdom, and wisdom is the crown point of the upper triangle, which represents the higher self or higher plane. Begin reading this triangle by turning up the rune representing wisdom (B),

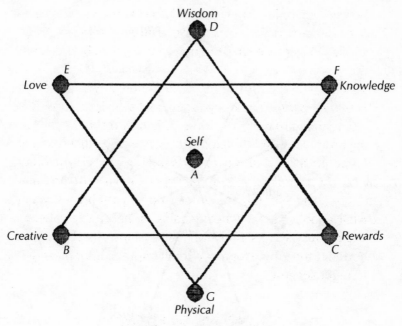

The Star of David
or
As Above, So Below
FIGURE 18

then the rune representing the creative energy wisdom generates (C) and finally the rune representing the rewards this energy produces (D).

THE GROUNDPOINT

As with several of these patterns, the Cross (see Figure 19) forms a mandala, and by meditating on the runes that form it, you can find your center or groundpoint in any situation.

The Cross designates the four seasons of the year—spring, summer, autumn and winter; the four elements—water, fire, earth and air; and the four directions—north, south, east

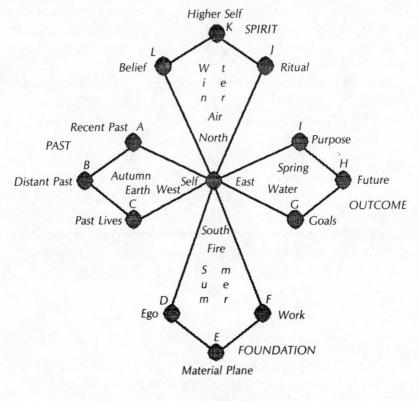

The Cross
or
Groundpoint
FIGURE 19

and west. The Cross can answer questions pertaining to a yearly (seasonal) cycle, including both past and future, and about the spiritual and material elements in yourself.

Choose thirteen stones at random and place the first stone face-down in the center to represent the Self. Place the rest face-down around the circle, beginning with the autumn cycle, to represent the past. Place the remainder of the stones on the rune cloth in the sequence shown in the diagram.

Begin by turning over and reading the central rune. Then turn over the three which form the left-hand arm of the Cross (A, B, C). These designate the past, which is composed of the recent past, the distant past and past lifetimes. Next turn over the three that form the lower arm (D, E, F). These designate the ego and the way in which it relates through you to the material plane and your work. Next turn over the three which form the right arm of the cross (G, H, I). These represent the outcome, which is determined by the goals you set for the future and their purposes. Finally, turn over the three runes at the top (J, K, L). These represent your higher or spiritual self, resting on a base of beliefs and rituals. Sometimes our beliefs get in the way of our rituals and vice-versa. Look for what the runes may be telling you about this critical balance and the role your higher self can play in maintaining it.

THE PATH OF PARADOX

Infinity (see Figure 20) is useful when you feel stuck in a mindset and your life doesn't seem to be going anywhere. It is also useful when stuck in a seemingly insoluable situation or when you are confused about some apparently contradictory element in life.

Choose seven runes at random and place each face-down on the seven spots shown in the diagram. Now in sequence turn up: (A) the past, an action or attitude which shows where you are coming from; (B) the ego, your present attitude or viewpoint; (C) the crossover, the turning point or neutralizing rune; (D) your resistance to progress; (E) the possible and/or eventual outcome; and (F) the lesson to be learned, or the solution to the paradox. Then reread (C) the crossover point, which forms the transition to (G) the unknown, perhaps something you are afraid of finding out.

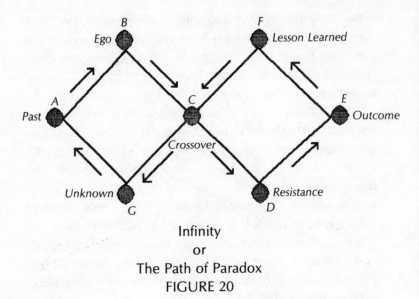

Infinity
or
The Path of Paradox
FIGURE 20

Now reread the entire layout once again until all the aspects and sequences of runes become clear.

If you contemplate the form of the paradox, the apparent duality will resolve itself and disappear. If you meditate on the form of your paradoxes long enough and detach yourself from them emotionally, you may even reach Satori.

MEDITATION

The Interlocked Triangles which make up this pattern create a harmonious mandala (see Figure 21). This argument is valuable when you are faced with a problem that requires an expedient but equitable solution.

Choose five runestones at random and place them facedown at each of the five positions. The two runes at the bottom (B, C), the feet, represent the base of the problem. The hands, the middle two runes (D, F), represent the means to manifest the solution, or the process for handling the problem. The rune at the top represents the head (A); look

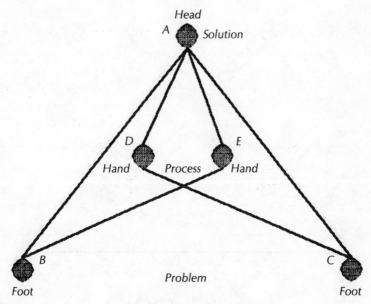

The Interlocked Triangles
or
Meditation
FIGURE 21

to it for clues to how your spiritual self can mediate the solution.

We can resolve our problems in many different ways, but when we resolve an issue in a spiritual way, we live in our own highest interest and in God's highest interest. When the two ways are blended as one, then we are living according to the Tao.

TRIFOLD TRANSFORMATION

Use the Triangle (see Figure 22) whenever there is a need to better understand a process of transformation in which you are involved.

Choose any three runestones at random. Place them face

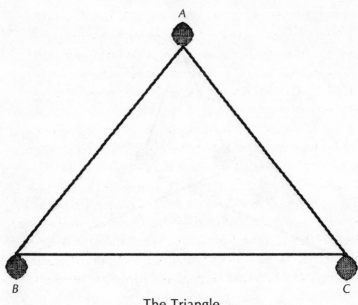

The Triangle
or
Trifold Transformation
FIGURE 22

down at each of the three points of the Triangle. According to the nature of the question, label them anyway you wish: mind, body, spirit; past, present, future; Self, ego, collective unconscious; Self, family, community. Turn all three stones face-up. See how each stone and the whole seem to relate to your transformational process.

GAME OF COMMUNICATION

This is an excellent way to use the runes to communicate with others, rather than solely as a means of communicating with your inner self.

If there are several of you, sit in a circle and have each

participant choose runes consecutively until all the runes have been distributed equally among the group. Any remaining odd runes are to be put aside until later. Arbitrarily divide the rune circle into as many wedges as there are people. You can do this using thin wooden skewers, for example.

Select one person to start. Whoever is chosen makes a wish and casts their stone into the circle. If it lands facedown, turn it over. Then have the person casting the rune describe it to the person into whose wedge the rune falls as if the rune were a wish. Have these two people discuss their reactions and how they feel the rune applies to their own lives. If the rune lands near the center, then the wish is described to the group as a whole and everyone discusses it.

Continue clockwise until all the runes are used up.

APPENDIX

SUPPLEMENTARY READINGS FOR INDIVIDUALS AND COUPLES

A. INDIVIDUALS

PETER CADDY

Peter Caddy is one of the original founders of Findhorn, a highly successful spiritual community in Scotland. Peter, who now resides in the Bay Area, radiates robust health, dignity, humor, wisdom and peace. I considered myself fortunate just to be in his presence, let alone to read the runes for him.

The following reading (see Figure 23) was done on the occasion of his seventieth birthday, as a life-like portrait of St. Germain looked on from above the mantle. Peter's rune reading was exactly what one would expect of such a man.

A straight line of runes, a line of power, courses through the Circle of Inner Being, moving outward into the Ring of Manifestation, or Ego Realm. The rune closest to the center is (ᛣ) Cen, the path, which seems to be moving straight up. Just above it is (ᚫ) Aesc, transformation, face-up but covered by (ᚾ) Nyd, constraint, face-down.

Peter seemed centered on his path, but the runes indicated that his life was about to go through another transformation. However, (ᚾ) Nyd represented only a temporary

RUNE DIAGRAM

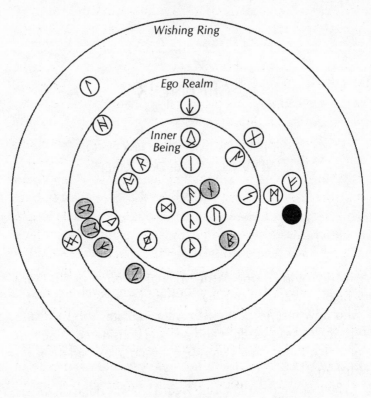

Peter Caddy
FIGURE 23

obstruction in his path. It was also a sign that there was no
reason to worry, that everything would happen at the right
time. Just above (ᚾ) *Nyd* is (ᛁ) *Is*, clarity, vision, and above
that, (ᛟ) *Ethel*, home, crowned by (ᛏ) *Tir*, faith. This sequence seemed to suggest that instead of worrying about
the obstacles blocking his path, Peter should keep his eyes
on the higher goals that were his vision and have faith in
his home. I wondered if this meant Findhorn, but Peter said

that he wanted to move up onto Mt. Tamalpais, the wonderful magical goddess-mountain in Marin County.

At the bottom of his Inner Being, below (ᚲ) *Cen*, is (ᚦ) *Thorn*, pointing to (ᚷ) *Ger*, abundance. I felt this indicated that Peter might be about to become involved in some big global issue frought with difficulties. Next to (ᚲ) *Cen* is (ᛞ) *Daeg*, meditation, which suggested one way of staying focused during all this effort.

(ᚹ) *Wynn*, joy, radiates into the Circle of Manifestation, followed by three runes, all face-down. In the middle was (ᛗ) *Eh*, work, which to me seemed inward—not at a standstill, but waiting for something to happen. Surrounding work are (ᛈ) *Peordh*, the fool, on one side—which I thought might represent the elementals, little plant Devas which helped make the Findhorn gardens such a remarkable success—and (ᛉ) *Eolh*, the Spirit Guides, on the other. I felt this was one of the most important configurations of the reading. In starting Findhorn, Peter's work was remarkably furthered because he learned to trust his Spirit Guides (St. Germain and others) and the elementals. The vegetables and flowers grown at Findhorn were remarkable both in size and variety, considering the soil and cold weather of Northern Scotland. I felt that Peter's future work would be different, though similar to his Findhorn work; while (ᛝ) *Ing*, the hero, following (ᛗ) *Eh*, work, made me feel that he would emerge from it as always, the hero.

In the upper left portion of the Circle of Inner Being are the runes (ᚩ) *Os*, communication, and (ᚱ) *Rad*, travel. And sure enough Peter later showed me a travel brochure for a tour of the spiritual centers of the United Kingdom which he was about to lead.

To the right, in the Circle of Inner Being, is (ᚪ) *Ac*, free will, the oak tree. I did not know if this really meant free will and if the oak meant something special to him as it had to the Druids. In the Ego Realm, beyond (ᛝ) *Ac*, is (ᚷ) *Gyfu*, giving and relating. This sequence suggested that Peter is in control of himself and able to give of himself or deny himself to others, as the need arises. At the three o'clock position is (ᚻ) *Sigil*, the Sun, shining out from the Circle of Inner Being onto (ᛗ) *Mann*, the people (I felt this represented mankind), followed by (◊) the Wishing Stone and (ᚼ) *Feoh*, prosperity. Certainly Peter's deepest wish is for prosperity for all peoples.

Coming from his center is (ᚩ) *Ur*, health, reflecting his own strength and good health, followed by (ᛒ) *Beorc*, the feminine, face-down. Just inside the Ring of Manifestation, at the bottom, is (ᛁ) *Eoh*, the masculine energy, also face-down. This indicated to me that both of these processes were directed inward at the time of Peter's reading.

In the upper left side of his Ego Realm is (ᚾ) *Haegl*, opportunities, and a wish in the Wishing Ring for (ᛁ) *Lagu*, love—once again indicating this wonderful man's wish for all of us.

KIRBY

Kirby (see Figure 24) is the mother of a young baby almost a year old. Although the two runes in her Center of Being are face-down, they nonetheless characterize her well. They are (ᛗ) *Eh*, work, and (ᛈ) *Peordh*, the child. Even so, they are only one part of the picture for her.

Just below (ᛈ) *Peordh*, is (ᛦ) *Eolh*, her Spirit Guides, watching over Kirby and her son. To the right is (ᚻ) *Sigil*, the Sun, shining on (ᛁ) *Eoh*, the masculine energy, which could be her husband, who gives her lots of support, or her own masculine energy, which seems to be in abeyance at the moment, as is a part of herself that wants to be out in the world again. From the Ego Realm, (ᛏ) *Tir*, faith, points to (ᛁ)

RUNE DIAGRAM

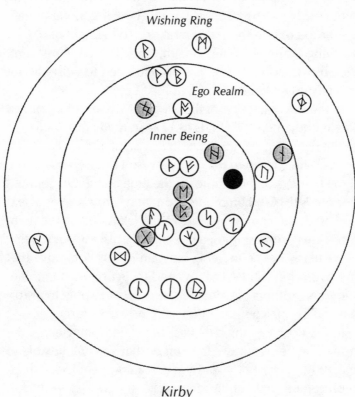

Kirby
FIGURE 24

Eoh and says to wait before venturing forth, for her child needs her now.

At the lower side of the Inner Being is a triangle of runes: (ᛚ) *Lagu*, love, (ᚫ) *Aesc*, transformation, and (X) *Gyfu*, for-giveness, suggest love and transformation through forgive-ness—a constant factor in any stable relationship.

Just above (ᛗ) *Eh*, work, is (ᚦ) *Thorn*, next to (ᚠ) *Feoh*, prosperity. This suggested that Kirby suffered from the illu-sion that she was not contributing enough to her family and wanted to seek new opportunities, (ᛡ) *Haegl*, to help them, but that her family members did not always understand her motives. Near (ᛡ) *Haegl* is (◊) the Wishing Stone, which seems to confirm this interpretation. To the right of (◊) the Wishing Stone is (ᚢ) *Ur*, health, and (ᛏ) *Nyd*, constraint, face-down, as a sign she has no real need to worry about her wishes or her health.

In the lower left side of the Ring of Manifestation, or Ego Realm, beyond (X) *Gyfu*, is (ᛝ) *Daeg*, meditation, and just to the right, (ᛤ) *Cen*, the path, (|) *Is*, vision, and (ᛩ) *Ethel*, the home. This suggested that Kirby's wisest course was to continue to focus on her home for the time being. On her midheaven is (ᛗ) *Os*, communication, and Kirby is a very clear and articulate communicator. To the left is (ᛥ) *Ing*, the hero, face-down, representing her feeling that she was not being particularly heroic in being only a mother. But above that are two runes, (ᚹ) *Wynn*, joy, and (ᛒ) *Beorc*, the feminine. "Joyous Mothers" is a name she wants to apply to an organization for young mothers she hopes to form.

In the Wishing Ring is (ᚱ) *Rad*, travel, indicating either the hope that her work will take off or that she will be able to travel with her work. Nearby is (ᛗ) *Mann*, people—perhaps representing her family or people she will meet in her travels. At polar opposites to each other are two other wishes: at the lower left, (ᛉ) *Ac*, free will, which I guessed represented the need all young mothers have for something of their own, and (ᛂ) *Ger*, abundance, representing Kirby's feelings about the child in her life.

JOY

Joy's reading was also done as a birthday reading. It is interesting that most of Joy's runes (see Figure 25) landed just outside the Circle of Inner Being. Joy is an extroverted and highly creative person who works as a quilter, fabric designer and rubber-stamp artist.

In the Center of Being is (Þ) *Thorn*, but for someone of Joy's character the thorns, like all difficulties, almost always represent creative opportunities. Her typical reply to a thorny situation is, "How can I make money with it?" She is a true entrepreneur. Moving upward and to the left is (ᛁ) *Eoh*, the masculine energy, and just beyond, (X) *Gyfu*, relationship, and (ᚾ) *Lagu*, love. This configuration suggested

RUNE DIAGRAM

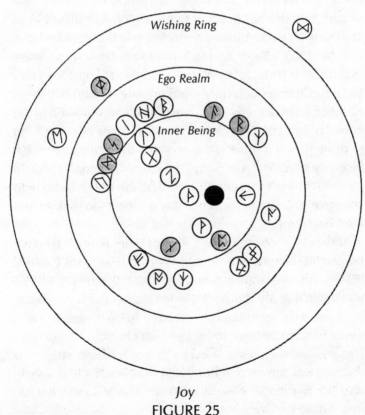

Joy
FIGURE 25

Joy's boyfriend, whom she loves very much and with whom she shares a home.

Also in the Circle of Inner Being, a little below the center, is (Þ) *Wynn*, joy. This rune is almost always close to Joy's center in every reading I have done for her. Next to it and face-down is (K) *Peordh*, the creative child. This is very much who Joy is—the creative child, always in the process of some new creation. Next to (Þ) *the Thorn*, are (◊) the Wishing Stone and (↑) *Tir*, faith, indicating that hope and faith are very much a part of her deepest being.

Surrounding (Γ) *Lagu*, love, are (N) *Haegl*, opportunity, (ß) *Beorc*, the feminine, and (|) *Is*, her vision, indicating a new perspective she has brought to life which will allow her to see the fresh opportunities opening up in the world around her. Next to (ß) *Beorc* and face-down are (Ⱶ) *Aesc*, transformation, and (R) *Rad*, travel, followed by (Y) *Eolh*, the Spirit Guides. Changes certainly seem in store for Joy, but she is not yet aware of them—they are future potentials still in the hands of her Spirit Guides. There is another configuration of three runes opposite this, in which the first two are also face-down: (ʮ) *Sigil*, the Sun, (M) *Mann*, the people, and (Π) *Ur*, health. I felt these indicated that she might be wise to conserve her energies and not spread herself so thin, to prevent impairing her health.

At the very bottom of the Circle of Inner Being is (ᚾ) *Nyd*, constraint, face-down, next to (Y) *Eolh*, the Spirit Guides, (Ⱶ) *Os*, communication, and (Ⱶ) *Feoh*, prosperity. I felt this was a sign that Joy should not worry, as her guides were taking care of things and all she needed to do to ensure prosperity was to continue to be her own charming, open self. Nearby, (◊) *Ethel*, home, next to (ᛉ) *Ing*, the hero, suggested that she was the hero in her own home—and she is, as she also is in her studio. Nearby is (Ⱶ) *Ac*, indicating that Joy has free will in her life.

In the Wishing Ring is (♦) *Ger*, representing a wish for abundance, and (M) *Eh*, representing her wish for more work. (⋈) *Daeg*, meditation, lies off the cloth, another apt symbol for Joy, whose lot is not to sit and meditate, but to be out doing and acting.

JULIE

Julie is a young woman I met recently who was in the process of seeking work and exploring different occupational goals. She had a young son who was not living with her at this time whom she missed very much.

In the Center of Being is (◊) the Wishing Stone (see Figure 26). I told Julie that she could make anything happen—all she had to do was believe in herself. The runes were cast in a way that gave her a lot of space: everything seemed to be scattered evenly in the Circle of Inner Being, and there were some interesting constellations in her Ego Realm.

Surrounding the Wishing Stone, in the upper portion of the Circle of Being, are two triangles of runes. The ones to the right are (∩) *Ur*, health, (Γ) *Lagu*, love, and (R) *Rad*, travel, change. This told me that Julie was in the process of improving her health and energy, and that while there was love in her life, it was somewhat suppressed at present. Julie was also hoping to travel, but the time was not yet right. However, next to (R) *Rad*, travel, is (N) *Haegl*, opportunity, so it looked like it would not be much longer before her wish would be fulfilled.

In the upper left side of the Circle of Being are the runes (F) *Aesc*, transformation, (◊) *Ethel*, home, and (♦) *Ger*, abundance. These reflect her inner effort to transform her home life and bring about abundance by finding a new job. In the lower portion of the inner circle are (Γ) *Ac*, free-will, and (M) *Mann*, the people, both face-down, indicating that Julie

RUNE DIAGRAM

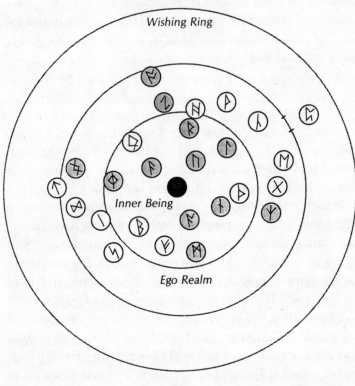

Julie
FIGURE 26

felt she wasn't interacting with others as effectively as she
wanted. To the left of these is (ᚠ) *Feoh*, prosperity, and (ᛒ)
Beorc, the feminine, both face-up, suggesting her great
potential. Julie could literally pull herself up by her boot-
straps, creating her own prosperity, if she so desired. To the
right of (ᚨ) *Ac* are (ᚾ) *Nyd*, constraint, face-down, and (ᚦ)
Thorn face-up. This suggested that Julie did not need to
worry about the thorns in her life.

In the Ring of Manifestation, or Ego Realm, outward from

(Þ) *Thorn*, are (Y) *Eolh*, the Spirit Guides, (X) *Gyfu*, relationship, and (M) *Eh*, work. I told Julie this meant her guides were actively directing her in her search for work (which was why she didn't need to worry) and to just let things work themselves out. Another constellation in the lower left side of the Ego Realm, is made up of five runes: (Ч) *Sigil*, the Sun, (|) *Is*, the vision or viewpoint, (⋈) *Daeg*, meditation, (↑) *Tir*, faith, and (ᛝ) *Ing*, the hero, face-down. All are close to (ᛒ) *Beorc*, the feminine. These runes represented Julie's positive energy, and I felt that she would emerge the hero if she could only learn to trust in herself.

At the top of the Ego Realm are two runes, face-down but near each other: (ᛇ) *Eoh*, the masculine energy, followed by (ᛗ) *Os*, communication. According to Julie, she was having a difficult time communicating with her child's father at the time. To the right, in the Ego Realm, are (Þ) *Wynn*, joy, and (ᚲ) *Cen*, the path, indicating that Julie was about to embark on a joyous path. Interestingly, (ᛈ) *Peordh*, representing the child, obviously her son, is in the Wishing Ring—just beyond the gates, so to speak. Julie told me that he was not living with her at the time and that the reason she wanted a better job was so she could afford to have him back with her. This may have been the joyous path she was about to enter, since it seemed to lead to her son. This may also be why (M) *Eh*, her work, is so close to the opening. It too seems to be a stepping stone, leading to her son.

MANIA

Mania is an extremely positive, highly capable woman who works in a job evaluation program. When she cast the runes, the majority landed face-up and the whole formed a very interesting pattern (see Figure 27).

To begin with, none of the runes have landed in the

RUNE DIAGRAM

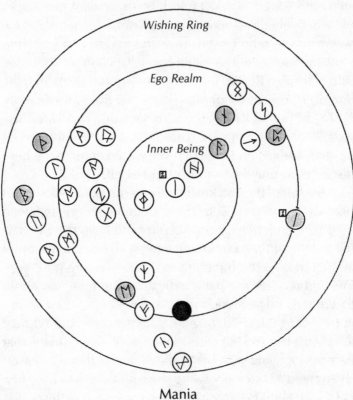

Mania
FIGURE 27

Center of the Inner Being, while (|) *Is*, vision, is face-down in the opening between the Ring of Manifestation and the Wishing Ring, like an eye looking into the beyond, but one that is closed and can see nothing. At the end of the reading, when I gave Mania a chance to place this rune anywhere she wished, she decided it really belonged in the very center and placed it there, connecting (◊) *Ger*, abundance, on one side and (ᚼ) *Haegl*, opportunity, on the other.

136

Beyond (ᚻ) *Haegl*, in the Ego Realm, is a triangular constellation of six runes, some face-down. The first is (ᚨ) *Aesc*,
transformation, leading to (↑) *Tir*, faith, (ᛈ) *Peordh*, the creative child, (ᛋ) *Sigil*, the Sun, (ᛜ) *Ing*, the hero, and (ᚾ) *Nyd*,
constraint, face-down. I felt this indicated an opportunity
for important spiritual and creative changes in Mania's life
that would transform her into the hero. (ᚾ) *Nyd*, face-down,
told me that she had nothing to worry about.

Also in the Ego Realm, but on the left side, are several
constellations which I felt represented Mania's past and
present. I saw a relationship with a man, (X) *Gyfu*, followed
by (ᛇ) *Eoh*, and that she had free will with regard to sustain-
ing it, (ᚪ) *Ac*. I also saw that this relationship brought joy, (ᚹ)
Wynn, to her home, (ᛟ) *Ethel*—all of which she confirmed.
Behind this group is (ᚩ) *Os*, communication, (ᛚ) *Lagu*, love,
and (ᚦ) *Thorn*, face-down. These told me that she was communicating her affections clearly to her lover, and that what
thorns there were in the relationship were not painful or important. Behind that, more or less in the Wishing Ring, are
(ᛗ) *Mann*, the people, (ᚱ) *Rad*, travel, (ᚢ) *Ur*, health, and
(ᛒ) *Beorc*, the feminine, face-down. This suggested an unful-
filled wish to take a trip that would allow Mania a chance
to relax and nurture herself. This she also confirmed.

Another constellation of runes lies across the lower portion of the Ego Realm and Wishing Ring: (ᛉ) *Eolh*, the Spirit
Guides, (ᛖ) *Eh*, work, face-down, (ᛥ) *Feoh*, prosperity, (◊)
the Wishing Stone, and in the Wishing Ring, (ᚳ) *Cen*, the
path, and (ᛞ) *Daeg*, meditation. When she told me that
some of the people in her office had expressed a desire for
a daily or weekly meditation session, I told Mania she was
a strong and powerful woman who would make an ideal
leader for such a group. This constellation seemed to also
say that everyone would benefit from these sessions, and
that everyone's work would become more productive as a

result. When Mania placed (|) *Is* between (Y) *Eolh* and (N) *Haegl*, I felt that she was seriously considering these daily meditations. However, she would have to take the steps to manifest it herself.

COUPLES

HEATHER AND PAUL

The following reading was done for a young couple who had been actively working to harmonize the various aspects of their relationship for the past three years and as a result appeared to be growing closer and wiser all the time.

In the Circle of Inner Being (see Figure 28) are a number of runes that show a strong spiritual connection with each other. In addition, one of the strongest lines of power in this circle seems to emanate from (ᛚ) *Lagu*, the emotion of love, face-down, and the three that follow, moving diagonally downward to the right. The fact that seven out of eleven runes in the inner circle landed face-down indicates the strong sense of privacy Heather and Paul share regarding their inner selves, and also that they are more focused on the outward, practical aspects of their relationship.

I began their reading with (ᛚ) *Lagu*. Next to it, also face down, is (ᛒ) *Beorc*, the feminine, and next to that (ᛏ) *Tir*, faith. It is clear that love is at the center of Paul and Heather's relationship, but that they both need to have faith in the feminine qualities which nurture love in the innermost being. Also in the Circle of Inner Being is (ᚹ) *Wynn*, joy, face-down, next to (ᛚ) *Lagu*. Beyond that is (◊) the Wishing Stone, and the wish seems to be for (◊) *Ethel*, a home of their own (they are presently living with one of their parents), and for (ᛥ) *Peordh*, children, face-down, next to the Wishing Stone. Also near (ᛚ) *Lagu* and (ᚹ) *Wynn* are (ᛗ) *Os*, communication, indicating that even though (ᚹ) *Wynn* and

RUNE DIAGRAM

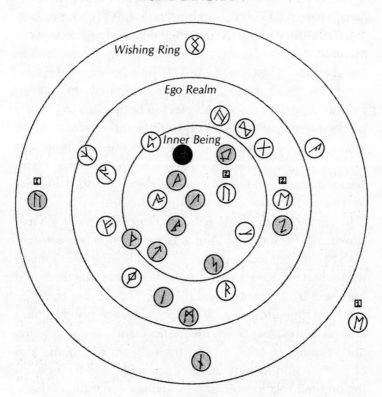

Heather and Paul
FIGURE 28

(ᛚ) *Lagu* are face-down, their communicaton is positive and outflowing.

Also in the Inner Circle is (ᚲ) *Cen*, the torch or lamp of knowledge, face-up, suggesting the deep certainty on which their relationship is founded. (ᛋ) *Sigil*, the Sun, is face-down, indicating a reservoir of inner energy which was not being tapped at the time. Beyond (ᛋ) *Sigil*, in the Ring of Manifestation, or Ego Realm, is (ᚱ) *Rad*, indicating possible travel or change, which might be the hoped-for change in homes, as neither planned a trip at this time. Next to (ᛏ) *Tir*, faith, face-down, is (ᚦ) *Thorn*, and next to that, (ᚠ) *Feoh*, prosperity. This cluster suggested that their financial problems were about to come to an end and that they should have faith in the abundance just ahead. Also (ᛏ) *Tir* is pointing to (ᛄ) *Ger*, which means abundance and lasting commitment, indicating the important place faith plays in both. Next to (ᛄ) *Ger*, but face-down, are (ᛁ) *Is*, clarity, vision, and next to that, (ᛗ) *Mann*, the people, family. These seemed to represent aspects of their relationship that did not require much conscious attention at the time, since Heather and Paul have friends and are both close to their families.

In the Ego Realm is (ᛇ) *Eoh*, the masculine energy, face-down. At the moment Paul was not completely satisfied with his present job or income. His skills were worth much more than he was earning and he felt somewhat frustrated and held back. Just beyond (ᛟ) *Ethel*, home, are three interesting rune groups, all face-up: (ᚻ) *Haegl*, opportunities and pleasures, (ᛞ) *Daeg*, meditation, and (ᛄ) *Gyfu*, giving and relating. In other words, their dream of a home and children could be actualized or strengthened by meditating on their relationship and by giving even more of themselves to each other.

To the left, in the Ring of Manifestation, are (ᚪ) *Ac*, the oak tree of "free will," and (ᛉ) *Eolh*, the Spirit Guides. This suggested that their guides helped them to make wise choices. Balancing these two runes, but on the opposite side of the rune cloth and in the Wishing Ring, is (ᚫ) *Aesc*, transformation, face-up, indicating their hope for a positive transformation in their lives.

Also in the Wishing Ring, face-down, is (ᚢ) *Ur*, health, indicating that there was little need for conscious attention to their health at the time. The two later moved this rune into the Circle of Inner Being, next to (ᛚ) *Lagu* and (ᚹ) *Wynn*. Just in front of them is (ᚾ) *Nyd*, constraint, face-down, telling them not to worry, that everything would turn out all right. The rune (ᛗ) *Eh*, work, has also landed face-down and lies completely off the cloth, representing their desire for a job change. When I allowed Paul to move any one rune he chose, he assertively took (ᛗ) *Eh*, work, and placed it near (ᛇ) *Eoh*, the masculine energy. Three days later Paul was offered a new job with an income twice what he used to earn.

On their mid-heaven, in the Wishing Ring, is (ᛝ) *Ing*, the hero, face-up, indicating Heather and Paul's desire to always be each other's hero and heroine. Paul quipped, "Honey, I'll be your Superman and you can be my Cowgirl!" And that pretty well sums up their relationship.

Cathy and Peter

Cathy and Peter, a couple in their early thirties, had been living together for eleven years and had finally decided to get married. They are a stable, fun-loving duo and have worked hard to become successful in their individual careers. Cathy and Peter truly mirror each other and even look alike. They held the runes and cast them onto the cloth jointly.

Most of the runes are in the Circle of Inner Being (see Figure 29), indicating that as a couple they have a rich inner life together. At the Center of Being is (ᛏ) *Tir*, faith, the core of their relationship. Next to (ᛏ) *Tir* is (ᚩ) *Os*, communication, and each of them works in the communications field. (ᛏ) *Tir* seems to be pointing to (ᚠ) *Feoh*, prosperity, and (ᚹ) *Wynn*, joy—two qualities I felt sure their marriage would bring them. Beyond these two runes were a group of three runes: (ᚷ) *Ger*, abundance, commitment, (ᚻ) *Haegl*, opportunity, and (ᛟ) *Ethel*, home. This configuration suggested that they could have a joyous and prosperous marriage and an abundant home.

RUNE DIAGRAM

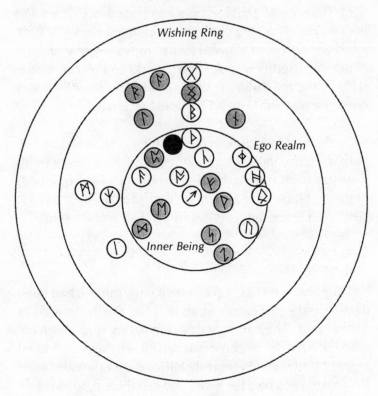

Cathy and Peter
FIGURE 29

Behind (↑) *Tir* is (ᛗ) *Eh*, their work, face-down, and be-hind that is (ᛞ) *Daeg*, meditation. At the time, Cathy and Peter were relocating to another part of the country because of their work and were concentrating their energies on the move. Beyond (ᛞ) *Daeg*, in the Ring of Manifestation, or Ego Realm, is (|) *Is*, clarity of vision, indicating that they would somehow see their way through all the problems and challenges involved in the relocation. Also in the Circle of Inner Being, near the bottom, are the runes (ᛋ) *Sigil*, the Sun, and (ᛁ) *Eoh*, the masculine energy, both face-down. As the move would take them to a sunny part of the country and both were in traditionally masculine careers as business executives, I felt this configuration represented their present situation as contrasted with the potential that lay ahead. Next to (ᛁ) *Eoh* is (ᚢ) *Ur*, health, face-up, and both are in good health at the moment.

Near the Circle of Inner Being, just above (ᛟ) *Os*, is (ᚳ) *Cen*, the light guiding them on their path. It leads to a row of four runes: (ᚦ) *Thorn*, (◊) the Wishing Stone, (ᛈ) *Peordh*, the child, face-down, and behind that, (ᚫ) *Aesc*, transformation. Above (ᚦ) *Thorn* in the Ego Realm is (ᛒ) *Beorc*, the feminine, followed by (ᛟ) *Ing*, the hero, and (X) *Gyfu*, relationship. From this rather complex double constellation, I guessed that they would not only soon be married, but that they would also soon have a child.

The fact that (ᚦ) *Thorn* is so close to (ᛒ) *Beorc* suggests the impending changes for Cathy, while (◊) the Wishing Stone next to (ᛈ) *Peordh* and so near (ᚫ) *Aesc*, transformation, combines to indicate the nature of the change. This interpretation is strengthened by the fact that (ᛟ) *Ing*, who is also the god of fertility, face-down, seemed to be hiding in the wings.

Also in the Ego Realm, between (ᚦ) *Thorn* and (ᚷ) *Ger*, abundance, gestation, is (ᚾ) *Nyd*, constraint, face-down, telling them not to worry about the forthcoming child. Next to (X) *Gyfu*, at the top of the Ego Realm, are three runes, all face-down: (ᛠ) *Ac*, free will, (ᚱ) *Rad*, travel, and (ᛚ) *Lagu*, love, all of which told me that there were no problems they needed to concentrate on at that time.

The final two runes in the Ego Realm, (ᛇ) *Eolh*, the Spirit Guides, and (ᛗ) *Mann*, the people, seemed to be saying that their guides would bless them as they moved on in their life together and that they would make new friends wherever they went.

Cathy and Peter were married and moved to another state soon afterward. Within three months Cathy was pregnant. For the first few months her new job required her to travel quite extensively, creating stress and a subsequent shift in her work plans. Cathy's pregnancy also balanced the male-female energy in their relationship, as the runes had suggested. They are now joyous parents of a precious baby boy.

AFTERWORD

I hope you have found this book both informative and useful. If you found wisdom, all the better. And if this book caused you to look deeper into the mystery of your own heart and psyche and to celebrate that mystery, then my true goal in writing this book has been fulfilled.

When the runes were first put into my hands, I meditated upon them and asked what I was to do with them. My guides told me they were a gift of the Spirit, a teacher, and that I was to bring them back out into the world with Light. Some of my ideas are based more on speculation and in-tuition, but I do not apologize. Instead, I offer them as a humble gift, a way of sharing my own prosperity—where prosperity means "having enough to share."

In *Rune Magic*, I have shown you how to make your own runestones and rune cloth. However, if you do not wish to make your own runestones, or cannot, you may write to me at the address below for a current Rune Magic price list and availability of supplies. If you wish a set of special minted runic coins, or runic jewelry, that is also available. And for those of you who are interested in using the Rune Magic system on a computer, a software package for the Macintosh is currently available.

If, as you use your runes, you have any questions or comments or merely want to keep in touch with other "runatics," please write to me. If you wish to subscribe to my runic newsletter, please send me $5.00 for a year's subscription, or $10.00 for a lifetime subscription.

My continued blessings for your transformative journey into the light!

Deon Dolphin
P.O. Box 3
220 Redwood Highway
Mill Valley, CA 94941

CELTIC BENEDICTION

Deep peace of the Running Wave to you.
Deep peace of the Flowing Air to you.
Deep peace of the Quiet Earth to you.
Deep peace of the Shining Stars to you.
Deep peace of the Son of Peace to you.

BIBLIOGRAPHY

Bain, George. *Celtic Art: The Method of Construction*. New York: Dover, 1973.

Blum, Ralph. *The Book of Runes*. New York: St. Martin's, 1982.

Bolen, Jean Shinoda. *Goddesses in Everywoman*. San Francisco: Harper & Row, 1984.

Branston, Brian, *The Lost Gods of England*. London: Thames & Hudson, 1957.

Cook, Roger. *The Tree of Life: Images for the Cosmos*. New York: Avon, 1974.

Crossley-Holland, Kevin. *The Norse Myths*. New York: Pantheon, 1980.

Cunliffe, Barry. *The Celtic World*. New York: McGraw-Hill, 1979.

Dolphin, Deon. *Rune Magic*. First Edition. San Francisco: Dolphin, 1982.

Fairfield, Gail. *Choice Centered Tarot*. North Hollywood: Newcastle, 1985.

Fuller, Frederick. "Barbarians and Empire." *CoEvolution Quarterly* 38 (June 1983).

147

Graves, Robert. *The White Goddess*. New York: Farrar, Straus & Giroux, 1966.

Grimel, Pierre, ed. *Larousse World Mythology*. New York: Putnam, 1965.

Howard, Michael. *The Magic of the Runes*. Wellingborough, Northamptonshire, England: Aquarian Press, 1980.

Johnson, Charles, and Carita Spencer. *Ireland's Story*. Boston: Houghton Mifflin/Cambridge, England: The Riverside Press, 1905.

Jung, Carl. *The Collected Works of C. G. Jung: Psychology and Religion*. Bollingen Series XX. New York: Pantheon, 1964.

————. *The Collected Works of C. G. Jung: Civilization in Transition*. Bollingen Series XX. New York: Pantheon, 1964.

Longland, Stella, and Maryjane Osborn. *Rune Games*. London: Routledge & Kegan Paul, 1982.

Muller, Robert. *New Genesis*. New York: Image Books, 1984.

Nichols, Sallie. *Jung and Tarot: An Archetypal Journey*. York Beach, ME: Samuel Weiser, 1980.

Owen, A. L. *The Famous Druids*. Westport, CT: Greenwood Press, 1962.

Page, R. I. *An Introduction to English Runes*. London: Methuen, 1973.

Sharkey, John. *Celtic Mysteries: The Ancient Religion*. New York: Crossroad, 1975.

Shumaker, Wayne. *The Occult Sciences in the Renaissance*. Berkeley, CA: University of Calif. Press, 1972.

Spence, Lewis. *The History and Origins of Druidism*. New York: Samuel Weiser, 1949.

Thorsson, Edred. *FUTHARK: A Handbook of Rune Magic*. York Beach, ME: Samuel Weiser, 1984.

Titchenell, Elsa-Brita. *The Masks of Odin*, Pasadena, CA: Theosophical University Press, 1985.

Tolkien, J. R. R. *The Lord of the Rings*. 3 vols. Boston: Houghton Mifflin, 1965.

Wagner, Suzanne. *Matter of Heart*. Film produced and directed by Mark Whitney, 1985.

Walker, Barbara G. *The Woman's Encyclopedia of Myths and Secrets*. New York: Harper & Row, 1983.

Wilhelm, Richard, and Cary F. Baynes, tr. *The I Ching or Book of Changes*. Bollingen Series XIX. Third Edition. Princeton: Princeton University Press, 1967.

Wilson, David M. *The Vikings and Their Origins*. London: Thames & Hudson, 1970.

NOTES

NOTES

NOTES

NOTES

NOTES